JUST ONE COOKBOOK

ESSENTIAL JAPANESE RECIPES VOL 2

**RECIPES + PHOTOGRAPHY
BY NAMIKO CHEN**

Interested in learning more about
Japanese cooking?

VISIT US:

www.justonecookbook.com

Introduction

Konnichawa. I want to thank you for taking the time to read this cookbook and hope you'll enjoy the recipes I've shared.

It's been a tremendous experience sharing recipes with you on Just One Cookbook for the past 10 years. I have wanted to publish a follow-up ebook since the first one was released in 2013. Somehow eight years went by before I was finally able to pour my heart into this second book.

When I started Just One Cookbook as a hobby blog to share recipes with friends, both my kids were under five, and I was doing my best to juggle family life with this new venture. Looking back at the beginning - taking photos with a basic point-and-shoot camera, oblivious to lighting or "food styling" - I would never have imagined what JOC would become today.

125 million visitors and 1,000 recipes later, the blog has evolved into one of the most visited Japanese recipe sites in the world. But one thing that hasn't changed since day one is my passion to share delicious Japanese and family recipes with you. I want to thank you for your encouragement, your personal notes about your cooking journey, and the kindness you've shown me over these years. I also appreciate all the feedback on what didn't work, so I could keep learning and improving.

NAMIKO CHEN

As Japan became a more popular tourist destination, the awareness of Japanese cuisine grew as well. In the beginning, I wasn't sure what recipes I could share that readers would recognize and make. These days, I am really happy when I see emails from readers who request authentic Japanese dishes they have tried in Japan. All those wonderful notes from you gave me the confidence to share my obscure and lesser-known recipes.

This cookbook has over 90 recipes which I've carefully curated for those of you who want to start cooking Japanese home-cooked meals. They are my family favorites, the ones that hold dear to my heart, and I hope you will enjoy them too.

It's been an honor to share my recipes with you!

Contents

Noodles

Sushi

Japanese Party Dishes

Desserts

Condiments & Sauces

Additional Cooking Tips

Recipe Index

BASIC + PANTRY

Aburaage

Thin slices of deep-fried tofu pouches with chewy texture. Aburaage are most commonly used to make inari sushi, miso soup, and simmered dishes.

Aonori

Powdered dried green seaweed that brings a savory briny tang to a dish. Use it to sprinkle over okonomiyaki, takoyaki and yakisoba.

Azuki Beans

Small, red beans that are most often enjoyed boiled with sugar and mashed into a sweet red bean paste called anko. The paste is used as a filling in many Japanese desserts. The nutty flavor of azuki is equally delicious in savory applications like mixed rice.

Bamboo Shoots

Tender shoots of the bamboo plant. Fresh bamboo shoots can be found in the spring, but you can buy a vacuum pack or frozen packages year-round. They are delicious in ramen, bamboo rice, simmered or stir fry dishes.

Substitution: Canned bamboo shoots.

Crab Sticks

Kanikama or imitation crab, commonly used in sushi rolls as well as salads.

Daikon

Japanese radish. Daikon is known to be digestive for oily foods; therefore, grated daikon is commonly served together with dipping sauce for oily food, such as tempura.

Dangoko 団子粉

Japanese rice dumpling flour specifically used for making dango. If you can't find Dangoko, you can make dango by combining Joshinko (上新粉) and Shiratamako (白玉粉).

Dashi

Seafood based stock usually made from kombu (kelp), katsuobushi (dried bonito flakes), iriko/niboshi (sardine) or a combination of all or two of them. Dashi made with only kombu is vegetarian dashi.

Doubanjiang (Fermented Bean Paste)

A salty paste made from fermented broad beans, soybeans, salt, rice, and various spices. Available in non-spicy and spicy versions. It adds fragrance and a deep savory character to many Japanese-Chinese dishes.

Dried Shiitake Mushroom

Rehydrate in water and use as you would regular shiitake mushrooms. Reserve

the soaking liquid for stocks, soups, and broths.

Dried Wakame

Small pieces of chewy seaweed used in miso soup, salad, and sunomono. A quick soak in water helps to rehydrate the seaweed.

Enoki Mushrooms

These thin and long needle shaped mushrooms have a mild and delicate flavor. Mostly used in stir-fried, simmered or hot pot dishes.

Egg Roll Wrappers

Made with wheat flour, these paper-thin dough are used to make deep-fried or fresh egg rolls. Find them in the frozen section, and I recommend the Spring Home brand "TYJ Spring Roll Pastry".

Fukujinzuke

(Japanese Curry Condiment): A popular sweet relish that is served alongside Japanese curry. It's made of a medley of chopped vegetables such as daikon, eggplant, lotus root, cucumber and pickled in a soy sauce base liquid.

Substitution: Pickled sushi ginger

Ginkgo Nuts

Considered as delicacy and often used in Chinese and Japanese cuisine, or traditional medicine for their health benefits. Commonly used in Chawanmushi.

Gobo (Burdock Root)

A type of long, slender root vegetable that has many valuable health benefits. Before use, peel and wash them thoroughly. It's a favorite ingredient in many simmered dishes like chikuzenni and mixed rice dishes.

Substitution: Any hearty root vegetables like carrots, parsnips.

Green Tea Powder (Matcha)

A fine ground, powdered, high quality green tea, different from regular green tea. Matcha comes only from shade-grown tea leaves and is used for Japanese tea ceremonies and Japanese sweets.

Gyoza Wrappers

Wheat flour based wrappers used for pot stickers. Usually thinner and smaller than Chinese pot sticker wrappers.

Harusame (Japanese glass noodles)

Made of both sweet potato and potato starch, Harusame is a popular noodle choice for Shojin Ryori (Buddhist temple cuisine). They are wonderfully slippery and absorb flavors very well. An excellent gluten free choice. The Japanese version is usually thicker than the Chinese glass noodles.

Substitution: Korean glass noodles.

Hijiki

Available in dried form, hijiki is a type of wild seaweed grown on rocky coastlines around Japan, Korea, and China. It contains high dietary fiber and essential minerals and has been part of a balanced diet in Japan for centuries.

Inari-age

Savory, sweet and full of juicy mouthfeel, Inari-age are deep-fried tofu pockets (aburaage) that have been cooked and seasoned with soy sauce, sugar, and mirin.

They are specifically used to make Inari Sushi and Kitsune Udon.

You can buy store-bought Inari Age or make your own with aburaage.

Japanese Rice

Short grain rice, Japonica species. Varieties include Koshihikari, Hitomebore, and Akitakomachi.

Japanese Curry Roux

Made with fat, flour and curry spices as the base flavor, curry roux is the key flavoring in making Japa-nese curry. The boxed curry roux comes in a block that resembles a thick chocolate bar. But you can easily make your own curry roux with just 5 ingredients.

Japanese Mayonnaise (Kewpie Mayo)

Compared to European or American mayonnaise, Japanese mayonnaise is slightly tangy, sweeter, and creamier. For substituting with non-Japanese mayo, add 2 Tbsp. rice vinegar and 1 Tbsp. sugar in 1 cup of American mayo and whisk until the sugar dissolves.

Joshinko (Japanese Rice Flour 上新粉)

Short grain rice that has been dried, and ground down into flour, joshinko is used for making dango and zenzai. Since it doesn't include glutinous rice, the texture can be chewy and doughy compared to Shirat-amako.

Kamaboko

A type of cured surimi, Japanese processed seafood product. Kamaboko is made from white fish fillet pounded into a paste, mixed with a starch and molded into a variety of shapes.

Karashi Hot Mustard

Sold in powder or paste form, karashi is made of a mixture of crushed mustard seeds and horseradish. It is a lot more spicy than the yellow mustard! Use it as a condiment in oden, gyoza, and tonkatsu.

Katsuobushi

Dried bonito fillet which is shaved into flakes. The bonito fillet is boiled, dried, then smoked and finally cured with a mold. It is then shaved to use for making dashi, or as a garnish or condiment.

Kanpyo

(Dried Gourd Strips): Commonly used as an ingredient in futomaki, a traditional thick sushi roll, and other sushi menus.

Kaiware Daikon

These sprouted daikon radish greens have a strong peppery taste, and are used in salads, sushi or as a garnish.

Substitutions: Alfalfa sprouts, radish sprouts, or other microgreens.

Kirimochi

Dried mochi rice cakes that come in rectangular or round shape. To serve, cut them into your desired size and warm up in the toaster oven or oven until puffed up.

Komatsuna

(Japanese mustard spinach): Dark green leaves that are rich in calcium. They are excellent stir-fried, pickled, boiled, or added to soups and salads.

Substitutions: Mizuna, spinach, bok choy, napa cabbage or daikon leaves.

Kombu/Konbu

Dried kelp used for making dashi.

Konnyaku

Made from Konjac, a plant of the taro/yam family, it is cooked and consumed primarily in Japan. This medicinal food has been eaten for over 1500 years. Used in oden, chikuzenni, hijiki and salad.

Mentsuyu

Japanese soup base used in soba and udon noodle dishes. It's made from sake, mirin, soy sauce, kombu, and katsuobushi.

Miso (Red Miso)

A fermented paste of soybeans, barley or rice, and salt. Red miso is mostly made with rice and is reddish brown in color. White miso (shiro miso) is used mostly in Western Japan recipes where Saikyo miso is popular. It's sweet and used for marinating fish. Awase miso is a combination of red and white miso, typically used for soup.

La-Yu

(or Rayu) Japanese chili oil.

Lotus Root

Crunchy, delicate flavored, lotus root is an edible rhizome (root) of the lotus plant. It is widely used in Japanese and other Asian cuisines. Usually sold in sections, they are great for stir-frying, deep-frying, pan-frying and simmering.

Substitutions: Depending on the recipes, water chestnuts can make a decent substitute in cooked preparations.

Mirin

Sweet cooking sake. It's a rice wine similar to sake, but with a lower alcohol content (14% instead of 20%). Mirin tenderizes meats, adds a mild sweetness, and helps mask the smell of fish and seafood. It has a deep body and umami flavor.

Mitsuba

Japanese wild parsley. A popular herb used as a garnish.

Mochiko

A type of sweet rice flour made from glutinous short-grain Japanese rice. It is sometimes called Gyuhiko 求肥粉 or Daifukuko 大福粉. It yields a sticky and chewy texture that is suited in making Japanese pastry and sweets.

Do not substitute it with other glutinous rice flour.

Nagaimo

A type of mountain yams that can be eaten raw. It has a light color skin and hairy roots, and is used in Okonomiyaki, Tororo Soba, Tororo Gohan, etc.

Narutomaki

A type of kamaboko (cured fish). Each slice of narutomaki or naruto has a pink spiral pattern that resembles the Naruto Whirlpools between Awaji Island and Shikoku in Japan.

Natto

A traditional Japanese superfood made of fermented soybeans. It is usually served over rice with green onions, soy sauce and karashi mustard. Most commonly eaten as a Japanese breakfast food. Eating natto has many health benefits.

Negi

(Welsh Onion): Also called Naga Negi or Tokyo Negi, negi can grow to several feet in length. The white part has a strong onion taste, but it becomes sweeter once cooked. This part is used in many braised and simmered dishes as well as hot pot dishes. The green part is used as aromatics or garnishes.

Substitutions: Scallions/ green onions.

Nishime Kombu

Dried seaweed that is softer than regular kombu, so you can make a knot easily to be used in oden or other simmered dishes.

Nori

Dried seaweed pressed into thin sheets and commonly used as a seasoning or as a wrapper for sushi.

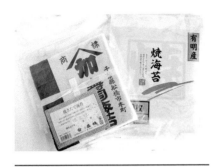

Pickled Red Ginger (Bein Shoga)

A type of Japanese pickle made from ginger cut into thin strips, colored red, and pickled in plum vinegar.

Okonomi Sauce

A sweet, tangy and savory sauce that is brushed over okonomiyaki. You can buy a ready-made bottle or make the sauce at home.

Ponzu

A dipping sauce made from a mixture of soy sauce, and citrus juice squeezed from daidai, kabosu, sudashi, or yuzu.

Quail Eggs

These pee-wee sized eggs have similar tastes to chicken eggs, but superior in their creaminess due to the high yolk ratio. They are a common feature in kushikatsu (skewered street food), and Japanese Chinese dishes like sara udon.

Panko

Japanese-style bread crumbs traditionally used as a coating for deep-fried foods like tonkatsu and Japanese croquette. They are larger, crispier, and lighter than regular bread crumbs and made of bread without crusts.

Rice Vinegar

This vinegar is made from rice and it is sweeter, milder, and less acidic than western vinegars. It is an essential ingredient in sushi rice and sunomono. Known

Potato Starch

Thickening starch. Can be substituted with corn Starch.

for its antibacterial properties, it is often used in Japanese dishes that include raw fish, seafood, and meat.

Sake

Pronounced as SAH-keh, not saki. Sake is made from rice and water through a brewing process like beer.

Sakura Denbu

A seasoned codfish condiment that is cooked, shredded, and dried to make flakes and are sweetened. These flakes are used as toppings for rice in bento boxes and Chirashi Sushi.

Satoimo (Japanese Taro)

Taro is a starchy root crop widely enjoyed in simmered dishes. Compared to other varieties, Satoimo is smaller in size and has a round body and hairy brown skin. Once cooked, it has a creamy texture and mild nutty taste.

Sesame Oil

Oil derived from sesame seeds. Besides its use as a cooking oil, it is also used as a flavor enhancer.

Sesame Seeds

White (shiro) or black (kuro) sesame seeds should be toasted in a frying pan before using to give off a nice aroma.

Shichimi Togarashi

Japanese seven spice is a mixture of red chili flakes, sansho (Sichuan pepper), sesame seeds, nori, and shiso, dried mandarin or orange peel, hemp and poppy seeds.

Shiitake Mushroom

Favored for its deep umami flavor and meaty texture, shiitake is the most popular mushroom in East Asian cooking. The fresh ones are great in stir-fries, noodles, soups, and simmered dishes, but the dried shiitake are preferred in making dashi soup stock.

Shimeji mushroom

Slender, tender beech mushrooms that come in brown and white varieties. They cook quickly and have a mild nutty flavor.

Shiratamako

(Sweet Rice Flour 白玉粉): A type of rice flour made from glutinous short-grain Japanese rice. Come in coarse granules and made exclusively in Japan, it is used specifically to make Japanese sweets known as wagashi. When you add the flour into the water, it dissolves quickly and yields a fine and pliable dough.

Shiratamako and Mochiko are both glutinous rice flours, and you'll find them being used interchangeably in recipes. However, there is an obvious difference between the flours when it comes to flavor and texture.

Shirasu

(Baby Sardines): Rich in calcium and protein, shirasu are used as a topping on chilled tofu (hiyayakko), and tamago tofu, or mix in with rice or rice balls. They are called differently based on how they are processed.

Shirataki Noodles

Thin, chewy, translucent, gelatinous noodles made from konnyaku (konjac yam). Because it is gluten-free, Shirataki is becoming more common in American grocery stores. The noodles have a mild texture after a good rinse.

Shiso

Perilla leaf. Member of mint family and has a slight basil-like flavor.

Shungiku

(Chrysanthemum Leaves): Sweet and slightly crunchy, these green leaves are a common addition to hot pots like sukiyaki and shabu-shabu, and are also very good in soups and salads.

Soba

A type of thin noodle made from buckwheat flour. Soba noodles are served either chilled with a dipping sauce or in hot broth as a noodle soup. Noodle shops in Japan usually offer soba or udon for options.

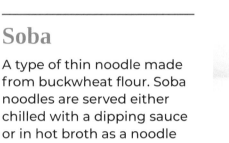

Soy Sauce (Shoyu)

Koikuchi shoyu is most widely used and may not be labeled but it is a regular soy sauce. Usukuchi shoyu is a saltier and light-colored soy sauce which is used when you don't want to discolor food material or sauce. Tamari shoyu is darker, thicker, richer and less salty than most soy sauce. It is made with no (or little) wheat and greater concentration of soybeans. This is a good option if you are gluten intolerant. Tamari shoyu is traditionally used to season sashimi, teriyaki-style grilled dishes, and longer cooking food such as soups, stews, and braised dishes.

Sushi vinegar

Seasonings added to steamed rice to make sushi rice. It's made of rice vinegar, sugar, and salt. You can make from scratch or buy from Asian grocery stores.

Sweet Red Bean Paste (Anko)

Dark red sweet bean paste made of Azuki beans. It is used in Japanese confectionery (wagashi).

Takoyaki sauce

The savory sauce that is brushed over takoyaki (octopus ball). You can use the bottled sauce, or make your own easily with basic pantry items.

Takuan

These pickled daikon radish are served in bento or at the end of a meal. They are believed to aid in digestion. Before eating, rinse off the excess brine and slice it thinly. Sweet, salty, slightly tart, and crunchy, takuan also makes a delicious addition to vegetarian/ vegan sushi.

Tenkasu

Crunchy tempura scraps of deep-fried batter. They add a fluffy and crunchy texture when added in Takoyaki, Okonomiyaki, or as toppings over udon/soba noodle soups.

Tobiko

(Flying Fish Roe): Tiny, bright orange eggs of tropical flying fish. They are served as a topping or garnishes for sushi rolls, sashimi, crab cakes, and seafood dishes.

Tofu

It is also called bean curd, made from soybeans, water, and curdling agent. There are many different varieties of tofu, including fresh tofu (silken/soft, medium/regular, or firm), fried tofu, and tofu skin.

Tonkatsu Sauce

A type of thick Worcestershire sauce mainly used as dipping sauce for tonkatsu and other fried foods like Japanese croquette.

Udon

Wheat noodles, available in fresh or dried form. They are favored for their big bounce and slippery chewiness. Usually sold frozen in Asian grocery stores.

Wasabi

Fresh wasabi is rare because it grows only in the wild and in cool shaded mountain streams. Outside of Japan, it is rare to find real wasabi plants. A common substitute for wasabi is a mixture of horseradish, mustard, starch, and green food coloring.

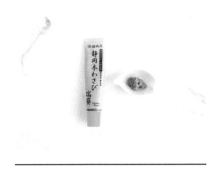

Yakisoba Noodles

Also called Mushi Chukamen 蒸し中華麺, they are made of wheat flour, kansui, and water. The color is yellow-ish, but they are not egg noodles. Look for fresh yakisoba noodles that are steamed and packaged. Alternatively, you can use dried ramen noodles when making yakisoba.

Yakisoba Sauce

In addition to Yakisoba noodles, this sweet and savory sauce is also great in any stir fries. You can use the bottled sauce or make your own. All you need is Worcestershire sauce, oyster sauce, ketchup, soy sauce and sugar (or honey).

How To Make Dashi

Dashi is the basic Japanese soup stock used in many Japanese dishes. Learn how to make Awase Dashi at home with umami-packed ingredients like kombu (kelp) and katsuobushi (bonito flakes).

 PREP TIME: 5 Minutes    **COOK TIME:** 15 Minutes   800 ml (3 ⅓ cups)

Ingredients

⅓ oz **kombu (dried kelp)** (10 g, 4" x 4" OR 10 cm x 10 cm)

1 cup **katsuobushi (dried bonito flakes)** (10 g)

4 cups **water** (roughly 1000 **ml**)

Instructions

1. Most Japanese recipes would say to gently clean the kombu with a damp cloth. However, these days, kombu is pretty clean so just make sure it doesn't look musty. DO NOT wash or wipe off the white powdery substance (mannitol), which contributes to the umami flavor in dashi.
2. Make a couple of slits on the kombu, which will help release more flavor.

OPTIONAL STEP: MAKE COLD BREW KOMBU DASHI AHEAD OF TIME

Put water and kombu in a large bottle and let it steep on the counter for 2-3 hours in the summertime and 4-5 hours in the wintertime. You can also cold brew kombu dashi overnight in the refrigerator.

TO MAKE AWASE DASHI

1. In a medium pot, add kombu and water. If you have cold brew Kombu Dashi (previous step), add Kombu Dashi and the hydrated kombu in the pot.
2. Turn on the heat to medium-low and slowly bring to a bare simmer, about 10 minutes.
3. Meanwhile, clean the dashi by skimming the surface.
4. Just before the dashi starts boiling gently, remove kombu from the pot (Discard or use for other recipes - continue reading). If you leave the kombu in the pot, the dashi will become slimy and bitter.
5. Add the katsuobushi and bring it back to a boil again.
6. Once the dashi is boiling, reduce the heat, simmer for just 30 seconds, and turn off the heat.
7. Let the katsuobushi sink to the bottom, about 10 minutes.
8. Strain the dashi through a fine-mesh sieve over a bowl or a measuring cup (Reserve the katsuobushi and see below for what to do with it). Awase Dashi is ready to use.

TO STORE

If you are not using the dashi right away, store the dashi in a bottle or mason jar and keep in the refrigerator for 3-5 days or in the freezer for 2 weeks.

WHAT TO DO WITH USED KOMBU AND KATSUOBUSHI

Save the hydrated kombu and drained katsuobushi to make Homemade Furikake (rice seasoning) or Kombu Tsukudani (simmered kombu). If you don't make them right away, you can freeze them for 2-3 weeks. You can also make Niban Dashi (see below).

OPTIONAL: NIBAN DASHI (SECOND DASHI)

1. In the medium pot, put 2-4 cups (2 cups would make stronger dashi) of water and previously used kombu and katsuobushi. Bring it to a boil over medium-low heat.
2. Remove the kombu just before the liquid comes to a boil, then lower the heat, and cook for 10 minutes, skimming occasionally.
3. Add an additional fresh ½ cup (5 grams) katsuobushi and turn off the heat.
4. Let the katsuobushi sink to the bottom and strain the dashi through the fine-mesh sieve.

How To Make Kombu Dashi (Vegetarian/Vegan Dashi)

Learn how to make Kombu Dashi, vegan-friendly Japanese soup stock, at home and create the umami flavor for your Japanese dishes!

 PREP TIME: 5 Minutes   **COOK TIME:** 15 Minutes   800 ml (3 ⅓ cups)

Ingredients

⅓ oz **kombu (dried kelp)** (10 g, 4" x 4" OR 10 cm x 10 cm) (You can add more for stronger flavor)

4 cups **water** (roughly 1000 ml)

Instructions

1. Most Japanese recipes would say to gently clean the kombu with a damp cloth. However, these days, kombu is pretty clean so just make sure it doesn't look musty. DO NOT wash or wipe off the white powdery substance (mannitol), which contributes to the umami flavor in dashi.
2. Make a couple of slits on the kombu, which will help release more flavor.

METHOD 1: COLD BREW KOMBU DASHI (MIZUDASHI)

1. Put water and kombu in a large bottle.
2. Put the cap on and let it steep on the counter for 2-3 hours in the summertime and 4-5 hours in the wintertime. You can also cold brew kombu dashi overnight in the refrigerator.
3. Remove the kombu from the bottle and reserve the used kombu (see next page). Kombu dashi is now ready to use. If you are not using the dashi right away, save it in a bottle and keep in the refrigerator for 4-5 days or in the freezer for 2 weeks. I recommend using it sooner for the best flavor.

METHOD 2: KOMBU DASHI WITH BOILING WATER (NIDASHI)

1. In a medium pot, put the kombu and water. [optional] If you have time, soak for 3 hours or up to a half day ahead of time. Kombu's flavor comes out naturally from soaking in water.
2. Turn on the heat to medium-low and <u>slowly</u> bring to a bare simmer, about 10 minutes.
3. Meanwhile, clean the dashi by skimming the surface.
4. Just before the dashi starts boiling, remove kombu from the pot (see next page for what to do with it). If you leave the kombu inside, the dashi will become slimy and bitter.
5. Now kombu dashi is ready to use. If you are not using the dashi right away,

save it in a bottle and keep in the refrigerator for 4-5 days or in the freezer for 2 weeks. I recommend using it sooner for the best flavor.

WHAT TO DO WITH USED KOMBU

Save the used kombu in the airtight container for a few days in the refrigerator or for up to a month in the freezer. With the leftover kombu, you can make Kombu Tsukudani (simmered kombu) or Homemade Furikake (rice seasoning). I usually save the leftover kombu enough to make tsukudani.

Homemade Miso Soup

It's super easy to make authentic Japanese miso soup at home! As the daily elixir of the Japanese diet, homemade miso soup is not only delicious, it also brings many great health benefits. Learn how to make this nourishing soup at home with my recipe tutorial and cooking video.

 PREP TIME: 10 Minutes   **COOK TIME:** 15 Minutes   4 Servings

Ingredients

FOR DASHI (MAKES SCANT 4 CUPS)
4 cups **water** (960 ml)

⅓ oz **kombu (dried kelp)** (10 g or 4" x 4" or 10 cm x 10 cm)

1 cup **katsuobushi (dried bonito flakes)** (10 g)

FOR ONE BOWL OF MISO SOUP (BASIC)
1 cup **dashi** (Japanese soup stock) (240 ml)

1 Tbsp **miso** (18 g)

Ingredients of your choice

green onion/scallion (finely chopped)

Instructions

TO MAKE DASHI (CAN BE MADE IN ADVANCE)
1. Clean the kombu with a damp towel and soak the kombu in water for 30 minutes or overnight (preferred). NEVER wash kombu and do not remove the white substance -that's umami! These days it's pretty clean, so you can skip this process. Just make sure there are no dirty particles.
2. After 30 minutes (or overnight), the kombu is re-hydrated. This liquid is called cold brew Kombu Dashi.
3. Pour kombu dashi and kombu into a saucepan. SLOWLY bring to a boil on medium-low heat so you can extract umami as much as possible. Right before the stock is boiling (it gets slimy and yields a bitter taste if you leave it), remove the kombu. Now what you have is Kombu Dashi. If you're vegetarian/vegan, use this kombu dashi for your miso soup. What to do with used kombu? You can reuse it to make Simmered Kombu or Homemade Furikake Rice Seasoning.
4. If you're not vegetarian/vegan, add katsuobushi and let it simmer for 30-60 seconds. Turn off the heat and let steep for 10 minutes.
5. Strain over a fine-mesh sieve and now you have roughly 4 cups of Awase Dashi. You can store in the refrigerator for up to 3-5 days and in the freezer for up to 2 weeks. Re-purpose the used katsuobushi to make Homemade Furikake Rice Seasoning.

TO MAKE DASHI (CAN BE MADE IN ADVANCE)
STEP 1 - ADD DASHI
You can use the formula; 1 cup (240 ml) dashi + 1 Tbsp miso = 1 serving miso soup. If you add more ingredients/vegetables, the amount of soup will increase and you will also need more miso. Add 2 cups (480 ml) dashi in the saucepan. In a hurry and no time to make dashi? You can use Dashi Packet or Dashi Powder to make instant dashi.

STEP 2 - ADD DENSE INGREDIENTS BEFORE BRINGING DASHI TO A BOIL

If your miso soup doesn't include dense ingredients or clams, go to the next step. Add dense ingredients like root vegetables. Once boiling, lower the heat and simmer until they become tender. If you're making Clam Miso Soup, add clams in cold brew kombu dashi. Bring it to a gentle boil and once the shells are open, turn off the heat (do not overcook).

STEP 3- ADD QUICK-COOKING INGREDIENTS AFTER DASHI IS BOILING

If your miso soup doesn't include these ingredients, bring dashi to a boil and go to next step. AFTER dashi starts boiling, add in soft vegetables like leafy greens, mushrooms, deep-fried tofu pouch because they require less cooking time. At this point, keep the soup at a simmer and make sure it stays warm (not OVERBOILING).

STEP 4 - ADD MISO

Add a small amount of miso at a time (you can start with 2 Tbsp miso for 2 cups dashi). Put miso inside a ladle and slowly add dashi into the ladle to dissolve miso completely. You can buy a miso muddler or a fine-mesh miso strainer which helps you dissolve miso faster. If you accidentally added too much miso, dilute the soup with dashi (or water). NEVER OVERBOIL miso soup because it loses nutrients, flavors, and fragrance.

STEP 5 - ADD TOFU

Add tofu AFTER miso is completely dissolved because you might break the tofu when mixing in miso. If you add chilled tofu from the refrigerator, miso soup would get cooler. Reheat miso soup until it is just hot, but NOT BOIL.

STEP 6 - ADD WAKAME & GREEN ONIONS

Add re-hydrated wakame (seaweed). I recommend re-hydrating dried wakame in a separate bowl of water to get rid of the saltiness, instead of re-hydrating inside miso soup. Add ingredients that do not require cooking such as chopped green onions, mitsuba, yuzu, and blanched spinach right before serving to keep the fresh fragrance and color.

TO SERVE

Serve immediately. Place on the right side of the table setting for Japanese meals.

TO STORE

In general, it's best to use up all the miso soup because the fragrance and taste will be lost as time passes by. Let your miso soup cool at room temperature (up to 4 hours - otherwise miso soup will be spoiled) and then refrigerate. You can keep for up to 2 days in the refrigerator. If you want to make a big batch, it's best to keep the soup BEFORE adding miso. Add the miso only for the portion you need. You can freeze miso soup for up to 2 weeks. If the miso soup contains potatoes or tofu, remove them before freezing as the textures subject to change.

TO REHEAT MISO SOUP

Bring miso soup in a pot over medium heat, but take care not to over-boil. Miso loses its nutrients at high temperature.

JUSTONECOOKBO

28

How To Cook Japanese Rice on the Stove

No rice cooker? Learn how to cook Japanese rice on the stove! My simple tips and tricks will ensure your rice comes out fluffy with intact grain each time.

 PREP TIME: 10 Minutes   **COOK TIME:** 15 Minutes   4 Servings

Ingredients

FOR AN AMERICAN MEASURING CUP (240 ML)
1 cup **uncooked Japanese short-grain rice** (240 ml)

1 ¼ cups **water** (300 ml; You should deduct 5-10% of water for sushi rice)

FOR A RICE COOKER CUP (180 ML)
1 rice cooker cup **uncooked Japanese shortgrain rice** (180 ml)

200 ml **water** (You should deduct 5-10% of water for sushi rice)

Instructions

TO PREPARE RICE
1. For Japanese short-grain rice, the ideal rice to water ratio is 1 : 1.1 (or 1.2), which is 10-20% more water. For American "cup" measurement, I used 25% for this recipe (rice to water ratio of 1 : 1.25). If you have a precise milliliter measuring cup or kitchen scale, use the following measurement. 200 ml water for 1 rice cooker cup (180 ml). 400 ml water for 2 rice cooker cups (360 ml). 600 ml water for 3 rice cooker cups (540 ml). 800 ml water for 4 rice cooker cups (720 ml). 1000 ml water for 5 rice cooker cups (900 ml).
2. Put rice in a large bowl. Rice absorbs water very quickly when you start washing, so don't let the rice absorb the milky water. Gently wash the rice in a circular motion and discard the water. Repeat this process about 3-4 times. Drain to a fine-mesh sieve and shake off excess water.
3. In a heavy-bottomed pot with a tight-fitting lid, put well-drained rice and measured water. Soak the rice for 20-30 minutes before cooking.

TO COOK RICE
1. Close the lid and bring it to a boil over medium heat. Take a quick peek to see if water is boiling (otherwise do not open the lid).
2. Once water is boiling, turn the heat to low and cook covered for 12 to 13 minutes, or until the water is completely absorbed (take a quick peek!). If you see there is water left, close the lid and continue cooking for a little longer.
3. Remove the pot (with the lid on) from the heat source and let it steam for another 10 minutes.
4. Fluff the rice with a rice paddle when it's done.

TO STORE RICE
Transfer the rice in airtight containers and close the lid to keep the moisture in. Let cool completely before storing the containers in the freezer.

Japanese Pickled Cucumbers

With just a few simple ingredients, you can make this crunchy and refreshing Japanese Pickled Cucumber to serve alongside your meal.

 PREP TIME: 10 Minutes   **COOK TIME:** 10 Minutes   4 Servings

Ingredients

2 tsp **kosher/sea salt** (I use Diamond Crystal; Use half for table salt) (0.4 oz or 10 g)

3 Tbsp **sugar** (1.1 oz or 30 g)

½ tsp **Japanese karashi hot mustard** (0.1 oz or 4 g; optional; You can substitute with Chinese mustard powder or Colman's English mustard which are made from a hot, yellow variety of mustard seed similar to Japanese mustard.)

3 **Persian/Japanese cucumbers** (9.2 oz or 261 g)

Instructions

1. Combine salt, sugar, and Japanese karashi mustard in the sealable plastic storage bag and mix well together.
2. Cut ½ inch off the ends of the cucumbers. Rub the ends together to get rid of bitter taste.
3. Put the cucumbers in the bag and squeeze out the air, close the bag tightly. Rub the cucumbers well with the mixture. Pickle for a few hours (my preferred taste) or up to 1-2 days in the refrigerator.

TO SERVE AND STORE

1. When the cucumbers are ready, discard the liquid and slice the cucumber before serving. Store the cucumbers in the refrigerator and consume within 2-3 days after removing from the pickle solution.

Shiitake Dashi

Aside from kombu dashi, shiitake dashi is another great option for vegetarians to make Japanese stock. To make flavorful and intense shiitake dashi, it is as simple as soaking dried shiitake mushrooms in water.

 PREP TIME: 5 Minutes   **STEEPING TIME:** 15 Minutes

 Servings: 1 DASHI (a bit less than ½ cup or 2 cups)

Ingredients

IF YOUR RECIPE NEEDS DRIED SHIITAKE MUSHROOMS:

3 **dried shiitake mushrooms** (20 g)

½-⅔ cup water (120-160 ml) (enough to cover mushrooms)

IF YOUR RECIPE NEEDS SHIITAKE DASHI:

3 **dried shiitake mushrooms** (20 g)

2 cups **water** (480 ml)

Instructions

HOW TO REHYDRATE DRIED SHIITAKE MUSHROOMS

1. Check if there are any dust or dirt trapped under the gills of the mushrooms, and if there are, use a pastry brush to clean. Do not wash it under water.

2. Ideally, you want to make shiitake dashi ahead of time. Place the mushrooms in a mason jar or an airtight container and pour cold water to cover the mushrooms. Let them soak in the refrigerator for a few hours or preferably overnight. However, if you are in a hurry, place the mushrooms in a bowl and soak them in warm water (body temperature) for 15 minutes or until softened. Put something heavy on top of the mushrooms so that they will be submerged under warm water and become fully rehydrated.

3. When shiitake mushrooms are tender, squeeze to drain, reserving the liquid.

4. Rehydrated shiitake mushrooms are ready to use. Remove and discard the tough stem of the mushrooms with a knife. You can use these rehydrated shiitake mushrooms as you would use fresh shiitake mushrooms.

5. Run the soaking liquid through a fine sieve (catch any dirt etc). Use the concentrated shiitake dashi for cooking, by steaming, seasoning, or adding into a sauce etc. No wasting!

6. If you plan to save for later, you can store in the refrigerator for 2- 3 days and 1 month in the freezer.

HOW TO MAKE SHIITAKE DASHI

1. Gather all the ingredients. Check if there are any dust or dirt trapped

under the gills of the mushrooms, and if there are, use a pastry brush to clean. Do not wash it under water.

2. Soak the shiitake mushrooms in 2 cups water. If you have time, let them soak in the refrigerator for a few hours or preferably overnight. If you're in a hurry, soak them in warm water for 15 minutes or until softened.

3. After soaking for several hours. When shiitake mushrooms are tender, squeeze to drain, reserving the liquid.

4. Rehydrated shiitake mushrooms are ready to use. Remove and discard the tough stem of the mushrooms with a knife. You can use these rehydrated shiitake mushrooms as if you use raw shiitake mushrooms.

5. Run the soaking liquid through a fine sieve and use it for cooking (this is the shiitake dashi). If you plan to save for later, you can store in the refrigerator for 2-3 days and 1 month in the freezer.

APPETIZERS

Fried Chicken Wings

Crispy, juicy, golden. These Fried Chicken Wings featured in Netflix® "Midnight Diner: Tokyo Stories" are a fantastic appetizer or snack to go with Japanese beer. Learn the simple tips to cook them right, and indulge in pure joy!

 PREP TIME: 15 Minutes   **COOK TIME:** 35 Minutes   4 Servings

Ingredients

10 **chicken wings**

¼ tsp **kosher/sea salt** (I use Diamond Crystal; Use half for table salt)

⅛ tsp **white pepper powder**

4 Tbsp **soy sauce** (60 ml)

2 Tbsp **sake** (30 ml)

¼ cup **potato starch/ cornstarch** (I recommend using potato starch for the best texture) (36 g)

3 cups **neutral-flavored oil** (vegetable, canola, etc) (for deep frying (720 ml))

1 **lemon** (for squeezing and garnish)

Instructions

1. Place the chicken wings, skin side down. Make 2 slits on the mid-joint of the chicken wings, avoiding the bone. Sprinkle salt and white pepper.
2. Evenly spread the salt and pepper on both sides of the wings.
3. Add the soy sauce and sake in a medium bowl and add the chicken wings to the marinade.
4. Coat the wings with the marinade really well and set aside for 15- 30 minutes.
5. Prepare a tray with potato starch. Coat each wing with the starch and dust off excess starch.
6. Heat the oil to 340°F (170°C) in a deep pot over medium-high heat (later on, lower to medium heat and keep it at the optimal temperature). Mix the oil and check the temperature using a cooking thermometer or cooking chopsticks.
7. Put the chicken wings (typical pots can take 4 max without overcrowding) and deep fry until golden brown, about 8-10 minutes, and the chicken's internal temperature is 165°F (74°C).
8. When the chicken is crispy on the outside and cooked through, drain the oil on wire rack or a paper towel.

Shrimp Egg Rolls

Deep-fried to golden brown deliciousness, these Shrimp Egg Rolls are a great appetizer to start your meal or a weekend party. Dip in a leek and miso sauce (Negi Miso) to enjoy!

 PREP TIME: 30 Minutes   **COOK TIME:** 15 Minutes   2 Servings

Ingredients

½ lb **shrimp** (roughly 10 shrimp, 227 g)

1 Tbsp **sake**

⅛ tsp **kosher/sea salt** (Use half for table salt)

1 knob **ginger** (roughly 1" or 2.5 cm long piece)

1 **negi (long green onion)**

5 **egg roll wrappers**

4 Tbsp **negi miso** (page 275)

¾ cup **neutral-flavored oil** (vegetable, canola, etc) (180 ml)

FLOUR MIXTURE "GLUE"
1 tsp **all-purpose flour** (plain flour)

1 tsp **water**

Instructions

TO PREPARE INGREDIENTS

1. Remove the heads and outer shells of the shrimp if they are still attached. Pull off the outer shell. Devein the back of shrimp with a skewer. The vein runs right along the back. Insert the tip of skewer sideways about ½ inch down from the head of the shrimp and pull the skewer tip up towards you. This will lift up the vein and you can pull it off with the skewer or with your hand. [Recommended] Clean the shrimp with a pinch of salt, 1 Tbsp potato/corn starch, and 2 Tbsp water in a bowl and rub until you see dirty water. Rinse until clean.
2. Cut the tip of the tail diagonally.
3. Remove dirty water in the tail by holding the tip of the knife down on the tail and squeezing the water out from the cut tip. If you skip this process, water retained in the tail might create splatter in the oil. The tail should be almost translucent.
4. Make a couple of slits diagonally underside of the shrimp. Hold the shrimp with both hands and straighten it as much as possible in order to get the desired shape.
5. In a small bowl, put the shrimp, sake, and salt and mix well together. Let it marinate until you're ready to use them.
6. Next peel the ginger and cut it into julienned strips and cut the negi diagonally into thin slices.
7. Cut the egg roll wrappers in half and peel off one egg roll at a time to separate them (now you have 10 wrappers!).
8. Prepare the flour mixture by mixing flour and water in a small bowl. Put the negi miso in a small bowl.

TO WRAP

1. Place an egg roll wrapper in front of you with one point of the long-side of the wrapper towards you. Place the negi miso and shrimp (tail sticking out ½ of the way onto the wrapper on the long side.

2. Put julienned ginger and negi on the shrimp. Fold bottom edge of the wrapper over the shrimp.
3. Fold the side edge over to meet the shrimp, and begin to roll.
4. Continue rolling until you meet the end of the wrapper. Place a small dollop of the flour mixture on the edge of the wrapper. Repeat wrapping until all shrimp are done.

TO DEEP FRY

1. In a large frying pan or medium saucepan, place ½ inch of oil. Heat on medium heat until hot and begins to have tiny bubbles when a chopstick tip is placed in the oil.
2. Slowly place egg rolls in the pan. Do not crowd. Cover with the splatter guard if you have one. Cook until golden brown and shrimp is fully cooked. About 3 minutes on each side.
3. Remove from pan and place on paper towel to catch any excess oil. Serve with negi miso.

Japanese Sake-Steamed Clams

Sake-Steamed Clams made in 10 minutes with just 5 ingredients! Sake brings out amazing flavors from the clams; simplicity at its best!

 PREP TIME: 5 Minutes   **COOK TIME:** 10 Minutes   2 Servings

Ingredients

¾ cup **sake** (180 ml)

1 knob **ginger** 1 inch, 2.5 cm (julienned)

1.5 lbs **Manila clams/littleneck clams** (de-grited) (680 g)

1 **dried red chili pepper**

freshly ground black pepper

1 **green onion/scallion** (chopped)

Instructions

1. In a large frying pan, add the sake and ginger and bring it to a boil.
2. Add the clams and a red chili pepper. Place the lid and steam on high heat for a few minutes until all the clams open.
3. Remove the lid and add freshly ground black pepper and green onion. Shake the pan to make sure the clams are not overlapping each other.
4. Serve clams together with the remaining sauce and enjoy while warm.

Vegetarian Gyoza

These Vegetable Gyoza are stuffed with a delicious mix of tofu, cabbage, carrots, and shiitake mushrooms. With golden crisp bottom, fresh juicy filling, and homemade dipping sauce, it's love at first bite! You don't have to be vegetarian or vegan to enjoy these Japanese pan-fried dumplings.

 PREP TIME: 30 Minutes   **COOK TIME:** 30 Minutes   80 Gyoza

Ingredients

FOR FILLING

12 oz **firm tofu** (340 g)

5 oz **king oyster mushrooms** (142 g)

2 oz **shiitake mushrooms** (57 g)

3.5 oz **red cabbage** (100 g)

5 oz **cabbage** (142 g)

1 tsp **salt** (for cabbage)

2 oz **carrot** (57 g)

3 oz **onion** (85 g)

2 **green onions/ scallions** (1.6 oz, 44 g)

1 knob **ginger**

1 clove **garlic**

2 Tbsp **potato starch/ cornstarch**

Instructions

TO DRAIN THE TOFU

1. Wrap the tofu with a paper towel and place it on a tray/plate. Put another tray/plate on top of the tofu and press the tofu down with a heavy object or two, for roughly 30 minutes to 1 hour (pressed for 2 hours; 400 g before pressing, 355 g after pressed). If you're in a hurry, you can alternatively microwave (without plastic wrap) for 1.5 minutes (W1000) and drain the water.

TO MAKE THE SEASONINGS

1. In a small bowl, add 2 Tbsp soy sauce, 2 tsp sesame oil, 1 Tbsp miso, and ⅛ tsp white pepper.
2. Whisk all together and set aside.

TO MAKE THE GYOZA FILLING

1. Discard the tough core of cabbage leaves and cut into julienned pieces.
2. Mince the julienned cabbage into small pieces. Depending on your gyoza wrappers, it's easier to tuck in smaller pieces in the wrapper than chunkier pieces.
3. Repeat the same for red cabbage. Discard the tough core of cabbage leaves and cut into julienned pieces.
4. Put the minced cabbage in a bowl and add salt. Rub the cabbage with your hands and set aside till it releases water.
5. Cut the carrot into slabs, then sticks, and mince them.
6. Mince the onion into small pieces.
7. Cut the green onions into white and green parts. Save the green part for garnish later and chop the white parts into small pieces.
8. Discard the bottom/end of king oyster mushrooms, cut them into sticks, and then mince them.

FOR SEASONINGS

2 Tbsp **soy sauce**

1 Tbsp **miso**

2 tsp **sesame oil**

1 tsp **salt**

⅛ tsp **white pepper**

FOR WRAPPING GYOZA

80 **gyoza wrappers**
(roughly; buy 2 Myojo
brand gyoza wrappers;
each package comes
52 sheets; you can also
make your homemade
gyoza wrappers)

Water (to dip and seal
wrappers)

FOR FRYING GYOZA
(FOR EACH BATCH)

1 Tbsp **oil**

¼ cup **water** (60 ml)

1 tsp **sesame oil**
(roasted)

FOR DIPPING SAUCE

1 Tbsp **rice vinegar**

1 Tbsp **soy sauce**

⅛ tsp **la-yu**
(Japanesechili oil)
(optional)

9. Discard the stem of shiitake mushrooms, cut them into strips, and then mince them.
10. In a large bowl, add the onion, two kinds of mushrooms, carrots, and green onions. Then add the minced garlic.
11. Peel and grate the ginger. Add 1 tsp of grated ginger (and juice if there is any).
12. Squeeze the liquid out of the cabbage and add to the bowl with all the ingredients.
13. Remove the paper towel and slice the tofu into thin slabs, roughly ⅛ inch thickness (pencil size).
14. Cut the tofu slabs into sticks and then cubes. Add the tofu cubes and the seasoning mixture into the bowl.
15. Mix all together. Once the ingredients are coated with the seasonings, add potato starch. Mix and see if they are still "watery". You may need to add more potato starch if necessary.

TO FOLD GYOZA

1. Prepare a tray/plate with parchment paper and sprinkle some potato starch (cornstarch). This will prevent the gyoza from sticking to the paper.
2. Take a wrapper and place it in the palm of your non-dominant hand. Use a teaspoon to scoop a small amount of filling and put it in the center of the wrapper. Dip one finger in a bowl of water and draw a circle around the outer ¼" of the wrapper with your wet finger until it's wet all around.
3. Fold the wrapper in half over the filling and pinch it in the center with your fingers (but don't seal yet!). Using your thumb and index finger, start making a pleat about once every ¼" on the top part of the wrapper from the center toward the right.
4. As you fold each pleat, press the folded pleat tightly against the back part of the wrapper using your other thumb and index finger. Make 3-4 pleats.
5. Continue with the left side of the gyoza. Start making a pleat from the center to the left.
6. Press the pleats tightly (make sure no air pockets!) and shape the gyoza to look pretty.

TO STORE GYOZA

Before the filling starts to release moisture to the wrappers, cover the gyoza with plastic wrap and "flash freeze" them in the freezer until solid (at least outside is frozen). Make sure to layout the gyoza flat. Once the gyoza is solid, pack them in an airtight bag. Because you flash freeze them, gyoza won't stick to each other in the bag. You can store gyoza for up to a month. When you use frozen gyoza,

do not defrost. Cook while frozen and steam for extra 1-2 minutes.

TO COOK GYOZA

1. Heat the oil in a large non-stick frying pan over medium heat. When the pan is hot, place the gyoza in a single layer, flat side down (in two rows or in a circular shape).
2. Cook until the bottoms of the gyoza turn golden brown, about 3 minutes. Add ¼ cup of water to the pan.
3. Immediately cover with a lid and steam the gyoza for about 3 minutes or until most of the water evaporates.
4. Remove the lid to evaporate any remaining water. Add 1 tsp sesame oil around the frying pan.
5. Cook uncovered until the gyoza is nice and crisp on the bottom. Transfer to a plate and serve with dipping sauce. For the dipping sauce, combine the sauce ingredients in a small plate and mix it all together.
6. Cut the green parts of the green onion and garnish, if you like.

SOUPS

Tonjiru (Pork and Vegetable Miso Soup)

Tonjiru is a savory pork and vegetable miso soup you can easily make at home. Packed with B vitamins, fiber and minerals, this healthy soup is nourishing and soul-fulfilling. You'd love it on a cold-weather day!

 PREP TIME: 20 Minutes   **COOK TIME:** 20 Minutes   4 Servings

Ingredients

FOR SOUP

10 oz **sliced pork belly** (272 g; Use at least ½ lb or 227 g of pork belly; for vegan, you can skip)

4 oz **gobo (burdock root)** (½ length, 100 g)

8 oz **taro (satoimo)** (3 pieces, 227 g)

1 **onion** (6 oz, 170 g)

9 oz **daikon radish** (2 inches, 247 g)

4 oz **carrot** (4 inches, 123 g)

½ block **konnyaku (konjac)** (4.5 oz, 128 g)

¼ tsp **kosher/sea salt** (I use Diamond Crystal; Use half

Instructions

1. It's easier to cut pork belly if it's slightly frozen, so put it in the freezer for 15 minutes before you cut. Meanwhile, gather all the ingredients.

TO PREPARE INGREDIENTS

1. Take out the pork from the freezer and cut it into 1-inch pieces.
2. Scrape the gobo skin with the back of your knife. The flavor of the gobo is right underneath the skin; therefore, you only need to scrape off the outer skin. Do not use a peeler.
3. From the end of gobo, make a cross incision about 1 inch deep. This helps "sharpening" the gobo easier. Rotate as you shave the end of the gobo, like how you sharpen a pencil with a knife. Soak the shaved gobo in water to prevent discoloring. Discard the dirty water and rinse gobo with running water.
4. Cut off both ends of taro and peel the sides with the knife (or peeler). Cut the taro into ⅓ inch slices and soak in water to remove the sliminess.
5. Cut the onion in half lengthwise and cut into thin slices.
6. Peel and halve the daikon lengthwise. Cut in half again (now they are quarters) and cut into ⅛ inch slices. If you have skinnier daikon, cut into thin half-moon-shaped slices.
7. Peel and cut the carrot in half lengthwise, and then slice thinly.
8. Cut the konnyaku into small and thin rectangular pieces.
9. Sprinkle ¼ tsp salt and rub well with hands. Let stand for 5 minutes. *Tip: Salt releases water along with the unwanted odor.*
10. In the meantime, bring a small saucepan of water to a boil. Once boiling, add the konnyaku. Cook konnyaku for 2-3 minutes and drain the water. *(Tip: This helps to remove the unwanted smell.)* Set aside.
11. Slice the negi diagonally.
12. Remove excess oil on aburaage with a piece of paper towel. Cut in half

for table salt) (for cleaning Konnyaku)

1 negi (long green onion)

1 piece aburaage (deepfried tofu pouch)

1 knob **ginger** (Need 1 tsp grated)

7 oz **medium-firm tofu** (½ of one package; cut into ½" cubes) (200 g)

FOR MAKING SOUP
1 Tbsp **sesame oil** (roasted)

6 cups **dashi** (Japanese soup stock) (1440 ml; for vegan, use Kombu Dashi)

6 Tbsp **miso** (Each miso brands/types taste differently, so please adjust the amount according to your miso)

FOR GARNISH
1 green onion/ scallion

shichimi togarashi (Japanese seven spice) (If you like to make it a bit spicy)

and thinly slice it.

13. Peel and grate the ginger. You'll need 1 tsp of grated ginger.
14. Cut the green onions into thin small rounds which we will use for garnish on top of the miso soup. Keep them in the bowl.

TO COOK TONJIRU

1. In a large pot, heat 1 Tbsp sesame oil over medium heat.
2. Add the pork belly and stir fry with a spatula.
3. When the pork is no longer pink, add the onion.
4. Stir fry and add daikon and carrot slices.
5. When ingredients are coated with oil, add gobo and taro.
6. Add konnyaku, aburaage, negi, and dashi. The dashi should be just enough to cover the ingredients. If not enough, add more dashi (if you have any) or water.
7. Stir to mix and close the lid to bring it to boil.
8. When boiling, lower the heat and skim off the scum and fat from the soup.
9. Cook, covered with the lid, on simmer until root vegetables are tender, about 10-15 minutes.
10. When an inserted skewer on a tough and thick vegetable pierces through, it's done cooking. Turn off the heat. If you are preparing ahead, stop here and let cool completely before storing the pot in the refrigerator.

TO SERVE

1. For the best flavor and fragrance, miso should be added right before serving if possible. Add 5 Tbsp miso using a strainer *(Tip: always start adding a little less than the recipe says; each brand/type of miso has different saltiness)*. If you don't have one, let the miso completely dissolved in the ladle first before releasing it to the soup. Taste the soup. If it's too salty, add dashi (if you have) or water. If the soup is not enough flavor, add more miso.
2. When you are done with miso, add grated ginger. *Tip: When you add tofu (always add tofu after miso as it is delicate), make sure your miso soup has a slightly stronger taste because the moisture from the tofu will dilute the flavor.*
3. Tear tofu into small pieces and add them. You can alternatively cut the tofu into cubes instead of tearing it. *Tip: Tearing add more surface of tofu which will absorb more flavor of miso soup.*
4. When you are ready to serve, reheat the miso soup on medium-low and keep it at a low simmer. NEVER let the miso soup boil because miso will lose the flavor.
5. Serve in the miso soup bowl, sprinkle green onion, and serve immediately.

TO STORE

Let the miso soup cool completely before storing it in the refrigerator. Consume within 5 days.

Kenchinjiru (Japanese Vegetable Soup)

Originally created as a Buddhist temple cuisine, Kenchinjiru (けんちん汁) is a clear soup cooked with root vegetables, tofu, shiitake and kombu stock. It's a well balanced, flavorful soup if you're looking for a meatless meal on a cold night.

 PREP TIME: 20 Minutes   **COOK TIME:** 30 Minutes   4 Servings

Ingredients

FOR DASHI
1 **kombu (dried kelp)** (1 kombu = 4" x 4" or 10 cm x 10 cm)

5 cups **water** (1200 ml) (for kombu)

3 **dried shiitake mushrooms**

1 cup **water** (240 ml) (for shiitake)

FOR THE SOUP
7 oz **firm tofu** (200 g)

½ package **konnyaku (konjac)** (130 g or 4.6 oz)

2 inch **daikon radish** (200 g or 7 oz)

1 **carrot** (100 g or 3.5 oz)

3 **taro (satoimo)**

½ **gobo (burdock root)** (100 g or 3.5 oz)

Instructions

1. Previous Night: Clean kombu with damp towel (paper towel). NEVER wash kombu and do not remove the white powder (that's where the umami flavor comes from!). Soak kombu in 5 cups of water overnight. If you don't have time, skip soaking.
2. Slowly bring the kombu water to a boil. Right before the water boils, remove and discard the kombu. Turn off the heat and set aside.
3. Put dried shiitake mushrooms in a small bowl and cover with water. Place a smaller bowl on top to make sure mushrooms are submerged.
4. Wrap the tofu with paper towel and place it on a plate. Put another plate on top to press the tofu, drain for 30 minutes.
5. Cut konnyaku into bite size pieces. You can use a spoon to cut konnyaku. By giving konnyaku uneven texture, the surface will absorb more flavor. Then boil for 2-3 minutes to get rid of odor. Drain the water and set aside.
6. Peel and cut daikon, carrot, and satoimo (taro) into slices. For daikon and carrot, I slice them thinly so it will take less time to cook. For satoimo, I cut into about ¼" (6 mm) slices and soak in water to get rid of slimy texture.
7. Scrape the gobo skin with the back of a knife under running water. Cut in half lengthwise and slice thinly. Soak in water for 5 minutes and drain.
8. When shiitake mushrooms are soft and hydrated, squeeze the liquid out and set the mushrooms aside. Strain the shiitake dashi into finely meshed sieve to get rid of particles and set aside.
9. Remove and discard the stem of shiitake mushrooms and

2 **green onions/scallions**

shichimi togarashi
(Japanese seven spice)
(optional)

Japanese sansho pepper
(optional)

SEASONINGS
1 Tbsp **sesame oil** (roasted)

3 Tbsp **sake**

½ tsp **kosher/sea salt** (I use
Diamond Crystal; Use half for
table salt)

2 Tbsp **soy sauce**

cut into quarters.

10. Heat a large pot and add sesame oil. Sauté daikon, carrot, satoimo (taro), gobo (burdock root) and konnyaku until the oil coats the ingredients.

11. Then add shiitake mushrooms. Tear tofu with your fingers and add into the pot (If you are using silken tofu, use a knife to cut and add it right before serving). Tofu will absorb more flavor when it is torn by hands. Sauté until all the ingredients are coated with the oil.

12. Add the shiitake dashi and kombu dashi and bring it to a boil.

13. Turn down the heat to simmer. Cook for 10 minutes, skimming occasionally. Use a fine strainer/skimmer to skim off the foam on the surface.

14. After 10 minutes, add sake and salt and continue to cook until the vegetables are all tender. Finally add the soy sauce.

15. Right before serving, cut the scallion. Serve the soup and garnish with scallion. Sprinkle shichimi togarashi and sansho pepper, if you like it spicy.

Japanese Clear Clam Soup (Ushio-jiru)

The classic Japanese Clear Clam Soup is made with kombu dashi broth and Manila clams. This light flavorful soup takes only a few ingredients and 15 minutes to prepare. It's traditionally served for Girls' Day (Hinamatsuri).

 PREP TIME: 5 Minutes   **COOK TIME:** 10 Minutes   4 Servings

Ingredients

1 lb **Manila clams** (454 g, 16-20 pieces)

4 cups **water** (960 ml)

1 **kombu (dried kelp)** (2" x 2" or 5 x 5 cm)

1 Tbsp **sake**

⅛ tsp **kosher/sea salt** (I use Diamond Crystal; Use half for table salt)

2-3 strands **mitsuba (Japanese parsley)** (for garnish)

Instructions

1. After you purchase manila clams, you will need to de-grit. Even though they are "ready to use", I highly recommend doing this process. Please see How to De-Grit and Clean Clams (page 279).
2. Gather all the ingredients (clams should be scrubbed and clean after de-gritting).
3. Put water, kombu, and clams in a saucepan and start cooking on medium heat. If you have extra time, I recommend adding kombu in water first to let it seep for a longer time.
4. When small bubbles form around the edges of the pot and water is almost boiling, discard the kombu. You can also skim the foam to make a nice clear broth. When boiling, turn down the heat.
5. When all the clams open up, add sake. Taste the soup and add pinch of kosher salt if needed. Clams will get chewy and hard when you cook for a long time, so turn off the heat and serve immediately.

Japanese Corn Soup

The Japanese love their hot or chilled corn potage and corn soup. This creamy and smooth soup will give you comfort as you welcome the cool evenings of late summer!

 PREP TIME: 15 Minutes   **COOK TIME:** 45 Minutes   4 Servings

Ingredients

4 ears **corn** (or 1.5 cans or 3 cups frozen corn)

1 Tbsp **extra-virgin olive oil**

kosher/sea salt (Use half for table salt) (I used total of 2 Tbsp kosher salt in this recipe)

¼ tsp **paprika**

½ **onion**

1 ½ Tbsp **unsalted butter** (21 g)

3 cups **water** (720 ml)

1 cup **milk** (240 ml)

1 cup **heavy (whipping) cream** (240 ml)

parsley to garnish

1 Tbsp **heavy (whipping) cream** to garnish

1 Tbsp **extra-virgin olive oil** to garnish

Instructions

1. Gather all the ingredients and preheat the oven to 450°F (230°C) degrees.
2. Slice off the corn kernels.
3. Place the corn kernels on a rimmed baking sheet, saving the cobs for later.
4. Add olive oil, sprinkle kosher salt, and paprika.
5. Mix all together with your hands and spread out evenly in a single layer. Roast the corn kernels at preheated oven at 450°F (230°C) degrees for 15 minutes. Once it's done, remove from the oven and set aside till Step 8.
6. Meanwhile, thinly slice the onion against the grain. Heat the butter in a heavy-bottomed pot (thicker at the base so it absorbs and distributes heat better).
7. Add the sliced onion and pinch of kosher salt and sauté until translucent.
8. Add the roasted kernels and water.
9. Add the reserved cobs in the pot as they naturally sweeten the soup. Push the cobs down to see if they are covered with water. If not, add more water.
10. Bring to a boil over medium heat. Cover and lower the heat to medium-low and simmer for 15 minutes. During this time I highly recommend skimming the foam on the surface for a more refined taste. After 15 minutes, discard the cobs.
11. Using an immersion blender, blend the soup until creamy and smooth. If you use a food processor or blender, let the soup cool for a few minutes before you start blending to avoid major splashes. Make sure to cover any opening with a towel when blending.
12. If you want to make your soup similar to corn potage (Japanese corn soup), strain the soup through a fine-mesh sieve

for a smoother consistency.

13. Transfer the soup back to the pot and add heavy cream and milk. The ratio is entirely up to you. I usually use equal parts of milk and heavy cream, 1 cup each. Bring back to a simmer and cook uncovered for 10 minutes or more, stirring frequently. Once the water evaporates and it'll be more flavorful.

14. Add kosher salt and freshly ground black pepper. Make sure to taste the soup when you season. I used roughly 1 ½ Tbsp kosher salt or so (I used up a total of 2 Tbsp kosher salt that I prepared for this recipe including salt I used for roasting corn and sautéing onion). Or individuals can decide how much salt they want for their personal serving.

15. Finely chop parsley. Serve the soup hot or chilled. You can drizzle olive oil and/or heavy cream and sprinkle the parsley to garnish.

Kabocha Soup

Delicious Kabocha Soup with just a few simple ingredients. Enjoy this rich and creamy soup by dipping with your favorite bread.

 PREP TIME: 5 Minutes   **COOK TIME:** 25 Minutes   4 Servings

Ingredients

½ **onion**

1.4 lb **kabocha (squash/ pumpkin)** (640 g)

1 Tbsp **unsalted butter** (14 g)

2 cups **chicken broth** (480 ml)

1 ½ cups **milk** (350 ml) (I use whole milk)

½ cup **heavy (whipping) cream** (120 ml)

2 tsp kosher/sea salt (I use Diamond Crystal; Use half for table salt)

freshly ground black pepper

TOPPING
parsley

Instructions

1. Thinly slice the onion.
2. Using a spoon, discard the seeds from the kabocha and cut into 6 thin wedges.
3. Remove the skin and cut into small equal size cubes.
4. Heat the butter over medium heat in a pot and cook the onion until soft and brown.
5. Add the kabocha and sauté to coat with butter.
6. Add the chicken broth and bring to a boil. Once boiling, reduce the heat and simmer for 12-15 minutes.
7. Using a skewer, insert into kabocha and check if it's fully cooked.
8. Puree the soup in batches in blender or puree with a hand blender until smooth.
9. Add the milk and heavy cream and stir till combined and do not let the soup boil.
10. Season with salt and freshly ground black pepper and stir over moderately low heat until it is hot.
11. Ladle the squash soup into bowls, garnish with the chopped parsley and serve.

SIDE DISHES

Hijiki Seaweed Salad (Hijiki No Nimono)

A classic Japanese side dish, Hijiki Seaweed Salad features a type of wild seaweed that is highly nutritious. It is simmered together with a myriad of vegetables in a savory dashi broth. The result is so full of flavor and perfect for meal prep.

 PREP TIME: 40 Minutes   **COOK TIME:** 10 Minutes   4 Servings

Ingredients

½ cup **dried hijiki seaweed** (1 oz, 30 g; 10 x more after rehydrated)

4 cups **water** (for soaking) (960 ml)

2 **aburaage** (deep-fried tofu pouch) (1.4 oz, 40 g)

3 oz **konnyaku (konjac)** (⅓ konnyaku, 85 g; optional)

3 oz **carrot** (½-1 carrot, 85 g)

¼ **lotus root (renkon)** (1.3 oz, 37 g; pre-boiled; optional)

1 Tbsp **neutral-flavored oil** (vegetable, canola, etc)

⅓ cup **shelled edamame** (2 oz, 60 g; cooked; optional)

2 cups **dashi** (Use Kombu Dashi for vegan/vegetarian) (480 ml)

SEASONINGS
4 Tbsp **mirin** (60 ml)

Instructions

1. Soak dried hijiki in 4 cups of water for 30 minutes.
2. Drain to a large fine sieve and wash under the running water.
3. Boil water in a small saucepan and pour it over the aburaage. This will remove the excess oil coated on the aburaage. Cut in half lengthwise and slice thinly.
4. Add water and konnyaku in a small pot and boil for 3 minutes to remove the smell. This also makes konnyaku absorb more flavors and improves the texture.
5. Cut the carrots into julienne pieces.
6. Cut the lotus root into thin pieces.
7. Heat oil in a medium pot over medium heat. Add carrot and lotus root and cook until they are coated with oil.
8. Add the hijiki, then konnyaku and aburaage. Mix all together.
9. Add the dashi and let it boil.
10. Add all the seasonings and mix well. Cook covered on medium-low heat.
11. After 30 minutes, add the edamame.
12. Cook uncovered to reduce the sauce until you see the bottom of the pan.

TO STORE
Store in an airtight container and keep in the refrigerator for up to 3-4 days. You can also freeze it for up to a month.

2 Tbsp **sugar** (Reduce the amount in half if you like; Hijiki Salad is typically on the sweet side for preserving purpose. Especially when packing it in a bento box, it tastes better as we eat it at room temperature)

4 Tbsp **soy sauce** (60 ml)

Kinpira Gobo (Braised Burdock Root)

Kinpira Gobo is a traditional Japanese dish often enjoyed at home. You might be familiar with it since it's typically served in bento box from Japanese markets.

 PREP TIME: 15 Minutes   **COOK TIME:** 15 Minutes   4 Servings

Ingredients

1 **gobo (burdock root)** (9.5 oz, 270 g)

⅓ **carrot** (7.5 oz, 70 g)

1 Tbsp **sesame oil** (roasted)

2 tsp **toasted white sesame seeds**

SEASONINGS

1 Tbsp **sake**

1 Tbsp **sugar**

1 Tbsp **mirin**

1 ½ Tbsp **soy sauce**

1 **dried red chili pepper** (optional; remove seeds and cut into thin rounds)

Instructions

1. Scrap off gobo's skin with the back of the kitchen knife. Then slice diagonally into thin pieces (about 2-inch length). Then collect some of the slices and cut into thin matchbox strips. Soak the gobo strips in water for 10 minutes, changing water halfway. After 10 minutes, rinse them under cold water and drain well.
2. Cut carrots into matchbox strips.
3. Heat the sesame oil in a large frying pan over medium heat. When it's hot, add the gobo and stir fry until 80% cooked through, roughly for 5 minutes.
4. Add the carrot and continue to stir fry until both carrot and gobo are tender.
5. Add sugar, sake, mirin, soy sauce, and chili pepper (if you add any). Cook until the cooking liquid evaporates.
6. Sprinkle sesame seeds and serve the dish into individual bowls or a large bowl/plate.

Simmered Kabocha Squash (Japanese Pumpkin)

Cooked in savory dashi broth seasoned with soy sauce and sake, this classic Japanese Simmered Kabocha Squash makes a great healthy side dish that is chock-full of nutrients.

 PREP TIME: 15 Minutes   **COOK TIME:** 30 Minutes   4 Servings

Ingredients

½ **kabocha (squash/ pumpkin)** (Small kabocha, roughly 1 lb / 450 g)

1 knob **ginger** (1 inch, 2.5 cm)(optional)

KATSUO DASHI
1 ¾ cups **water** (400 ml)

½ cup **katsuobushi (dried bonito flakes)** (6 g)

SEASONINGS
1 Tbsp **sugar**

2 Tbsp **sake**

2 tsp **soy sauce**

pinch **kosher/sea salt** (I use Diamond Crystal; Use half for table salt)

Instructions

1. In a small pot, boil 1 ¾ cups water. Once boiling, add katsuobushi.
2. Mix together and turn off the heat. Set aside for 15 minutes. Then strain the katsuobushi with a fine mesh sieve. Set the katsuo dashi aside for now. You can discard the katsuobushi or make furikake (rice seasonings) with the leftover katsuobushi.
3. Remove the seeds from the kabocha. Microwave for 2 minutes to soften the outer kabocha skin. You can skip microwaving if you have a sharp knife and the strength to cut through the hard skin.
4. Cut the kabocha into wedges, then equal 2" (5 cm) pieces. Remember, kabocha skin is edible and nutritious.
5. In a large pot, place the kabocha pieces, skin side down in a single layer.
6. Add dashi, sake, and sugar. Tip: Swirl the pot to mix the seasonings so you won't break the kabocha.
7. Cook on medium-high heat and bring it to a boil.
8. Add soy sauce and salt, and swirl the pot again to mix the seasonings. If the liquid does not cover ¾ of kabocha, you can add a little bit of water. Bring to a boil again.
9. Once boiling, turn down to medium-low heat to maintain the simmer. Cover with an otoshibuta (drop lid) and cook for 20-30 minutes (depends on size, and skin takes time to cook), or until the kabocha has a tiny thin crack near the skin (it's a sign for doneness!). If you feel the liquid is evaporating too fast, you can cover it with a regular lid (and you still need to use otoshibuta).
10. Remove from the heat and let kabocha sit covered (with a pot lid) until cool, about 30 minutes. This helps kabocha absorbs more flavor as it cools. You can serve at room temperature or reheat before

serving.

OPTIONAL GARNISH

1. Cut the ginger into a rectangular piece (so each strip will be the same length). Cut into thin slabs and then thin julienne strips. Soak in cold water for 1 minute and drain well. Set aside.
2. Serve with simmered kabocha.

Simmered Taro (Satoimo no Nimono)

Simmered Taro (Satoimo no Nimono) is a classic home cooked recipe that compliments the main dish in a typical Japanese meal. A humble yet wonderful way to appreciate the remarkable texture and pleasant sweetness of this starchy root vegetable.

 PREP TIME: 15 Minutes   **COOK TIME:** 35 Minutes   4 Servings

Ingredients

10 **taro satoimo** (800 g will become 700 g after peeling)

½ tsp **kosher/sea salt** (I use Diamond Crystal; Use half for table salt)

2 tsp **neutral-flavored oil** (vegetable, canola, etc)

yuzu peel (can be substitute with julienned lemon peel) (optional for garnish)

SEASONINGS
1 ¼ cup **dashi** (Japanese soup stock) (300 ml)

3 Tbsp **sake** (45 ml)

2 Tbsp **sugar** (26 g)

2 Tbsp **soy sauce** (30 ml)

1 Tbsp **mirin** (15 ml)

Instructions

1. Wash the taro with water and drain. Cut both ends and peel the skin. Taro will be slimy so be careful when you're handling with the knife.
2. Sprinkle kosher salt over the taro and rub with your hands. Then rinse under cold water and then drain completely.
3. Place the taro in a large pot and fill up with water until fully submerged. Bring the water to boil.
4. Once boiling, reduce the heat and simmer for 5 minutes, or until the skewer goes through. Pre-blanching helps to absorb flavors. Drain and remove the sliminess under warm water.
5. Heat the oil in the pot. Add the taro and quickly coat with the oil. The oil helps lock in all the flavors and umami inside the taro. It also helps keeping the shape without breaking into pieces.
6. Add dashi, sake, and sugar, and bring to boil. Skim if necessary.
7. Lower the heat and place otoshibuta (drop lid) and simmer for 5 minutes.
8. Remove otoshibuta and add soy sauce. Place back the otoshibuta and simmer for 20-25 minutes (depends on the size of taro). Lastly, add mirin and gently shake the pot to coat the taro with the sauce. Adding mirin toward the end gives a nice luster to the dish.
9. Optionally, garnish with julienned yuzu (lemon) peel.

Green Bean Gomaae (Sesame Dressing)

 PREP TIME: 10 Minutes   **COOK TIME:** 10 Minutes   4 Servings

Ingredients

½ lb **green beans** (8 oz, 227 g)

1 tsp **kosher/sea salt** (I use Diamond Crystal; Use half for table salt)

SEASONINGS
3 Tbsp **toasted white sesame seeds** (25 g)

1 Tbsp **soy sauce** (15 ml)

1 Tbsp **sugar** (13 g)

Instructions

1. Bring a pot of water to a boil. Even though your sesame seeds are pre-toasted, it's good to toast them again in a non-greased frying pan for a couple of minutes, gently jiggling the pan. Be careful not to burn them.
2. With a pestle and a mortar (or spice grinder), grind the sesame seeds, leaving some seeds uncrushed to add texture to the sauce.
3. Add soy sauce and sugar and mix it all together. The dressing looks more like a paste than dressing. Set aside.
4. If your green beans are not trimmed, snap the tip of one end of the bean with your fingers and draw it down the length of one side of the bean to remove any stringy fiber. Do the same thing with the other end, pulling it down the other side of the bean.
5. Add a pinch of salt and the green beans to the boiling water.
6. Cook the green beans for 4-5 minutes (3 minutes for French green beans/Haricots Verts) until they are bright green and tender but still crunchy.
7. Remove from the heat, place in a strainer, and quickly rinse them in cold water to stop them from cooking further (or you can transfer them to an ice-water bath). Shocking the green beans with cold water will help the beans stay green. You don't need to chill them; the beans should be still warm. Drain or dry well with a clean towel and cut them into 2-inch long pieces.
8. Transfer the warm beans to the bowl and toss them in the sesame dressing. Serve at room temperature or chilled.

TO STORE
Keep the leftover in an airtight container and store in the refrigerator for up to 3 days.

Japanese Cucumber Salad (Sunomono)

Need some cucumber inspiration? Try Japanese Cucumber Salad (Sunomono) in 4 ways! Marinated in vinegar, sugar, salt, and soy sauce, this sweet & sour cucumber salad makes a perfect side dish. It's light, healthy, and incredibly refreshing!

 PREP TIME: 15 Minutes   4 Servings

Ingredients

2 **Persian/Japanese cucumbers**

½ tsp **kosher/sea salt** (I use Diamond Crystal; Use half for table salt)

1 Tbsp **dried wakame seaweed** (2 g) (it will be 20- 30 g after rehydrated)

½ Tbsp **toasted white sesame seeds**

SEASONINGS
4 Tbsp **rice vinegar** (60 ml)

2 Tbsp **sugar**

½ tsp **kosher/sea salt** (I use Diamond Crystal; Use half for table salt)

½ tsp **soy sauce** (Use GF soy sauce for GF)

TO MAKE VARIATIONS (EACH INGREDIENT IS ADDED TO

Instructions

MAKE THE SEASONINGS

In a bowl, combine 4 Tbsp rice vinegar, 2 Tbsp granulated sugar, ½ tsp kosher salt, and ½ tsp soy sauce. Whisk well together. If the vinegar taste is too strong, you can dilute with a very small amount of dashi (or water).

MAKE SUNOMONO

1. Soak 1 Tbsp dried wakame seaweed in water and let it rehydrate for 10 minutes.
2. Peel the cucumbers' skin alternately to create stripes. Then slice them thinly into rounds.
3. Sprinkle ½ tsp kosher salt and gently rub them against each other. Set aside for 5 minutes. Salt helps drawing liquid from cucumber *(so that the liquid from cucumber will not be released after mixing with seasoning)*.
4. Squeeze water out from wakame seaweed and cucumber. Add them into the bowl with seasoning and coat well.

VARIATION 1 - CLASSIC:

Serve in an individual bowl or a large serving bowl. Sprinkle sesame seeds on top and it's ready to serve.

VARIATION 2 – WITH IMITATION CRAB

Cut 4 sticks of imitation crab into thirds and combine with cucumber and wakame seaweed mixture (from Step 4).

THE RECIPE ABOVE)
4 pieces **imitation crab meat (kanikama) (or real crab meat)** (skip for Vegetarian/Vegan)

2 oz **boiled octopus** (60 g) (skip for Vegetarian/Vegan)

2 Tbsp **shirasu (boiled salted baby anchovies)** (12 g) (skip for Vegetarian/Vegan)

VARIATION 3 – WITH BOILED OCTOPUS

Slice the octopus thinly and combine with cucumber and wakame seaweed mixture (from Step 4).

VARIATION 4 – WITH BOILED SALTED BABY ANCHOVIES (SHIRASU)

Combine shirasu with cucumber and wakame seaweed mixture (from Step 4).

TO SERVE & STORE

Serve in an individual bowl or a large serving bowl. Sprinkle sesame seeds on top and it's ready to serve. Enjoy! To store, keep in the airtight container and consume within 3-5 days (depending on other ingredients).

Japanese Potato Salad

Classic Japanese potato salad recipe. Made with mashed potato and colorful vegetables, Japanese potato salad is creamy yet full of textural crunch. If you're a potato salad lover, you will be happy to add this delicious version into your repertoire.

 PREP TIME: 15 Minutes   **COOK TIME:** 20 Minutes   6 Servings

Ingredients

2 **russet potatoes**

½ tsp **kosher/sea salt** (I use Diamond Crystal; Use half for table salt)(for potatoes)

1 **large egg** (50 g w/o shell)

2 ½ inch **carrot** (5 cm)

¼ cup **corns** (40 g)

2 inch **English cucumber** (5 cm)

2 slices **black forest ham**

¼ tsp **kosher/sea salt** (for cucumber)

⅓ cup **Japanese mayonnaise** (80 ml)

kosher/sea salt (I use Diamond Crystal; Use half for table salt)

Instructions

1. Peel the potatoes and cut into 1 ½ inch pieces. They should be roughly about the same size so that they'll be done cooking around the same time. Put potatoes in a large pot and add water until fully submerged. We start cooking potatoes in cold water so that it allows them to slowly heat up and cook through evenly.
2. Boil potatoes with high heat. After the water boils, lower heat to medium and cook until a skewer goes through the potato smoothly, about 10 minutes. Drain the water from pot and put the potatoes back on the stove again.
3. On the stove, evaporate water and moisture of the potatoes over medium-high heat (for less than 1 minute). Shift the pot in circular motion so the potatoes wont' get burnt. When you see no liquid left in the pan, remove from heat.
4. Mash the potatoes but leave some small chunks for texture. Sprinkle salt and transfer it into a big bowl and let it cool on the kitchen counter.
5. Meanwhile prepare a boiled egg. Remove the shell and mash the egg with a fork in a small bowl. Set aside.
6. Cut carrots into quarter (or half) and then slice it thinly. Put them in a microwave-safe container and cover it with water. Microwave for a few minutes until a skewer goes smoothly through the carrot (don't overcook). Drain water and cool down.
7. Peel the cucumbers (leave some skin on to create stripe pattern) and cut into quarter. Then slice it thinly.
8. Dice the sliced hams into small size.
9. Prepare and boil corn (canned corn kernels works as well).
10. Add hams and veggies into the mashed potato bowl. Grind

freshly ground black pepper

some pepper over and mix well.

11. Add mayonnaise and mix until incorporated.

12. Add boiled eggs and mix in gently. Let it cool and then refrigerate for 30-60 minutes before serving.

TO STORE

Keep in the refrigerator and consume it in 3-4 days.

Harusame Salad (Japanese Glass Noodle Salad)

Japanese Glass Noodle Salad (Harusame Salad) is light, refreshing, low calorie and so flavorful with a savory and tangy sesame soy vinaigrette.

 PREP TIME: 20 Minutes   **COOK TIME:** 5 Minutes   4 Servings

Ingredients

4.2 oz **harusame (glass noodles)** (120 g)

2 Tbsp **dried wakame seaweed**

1 **Persian/Japanese cucumber**

⅓ **carrot**

½ tsp **kosher/sea salt** (I use Diamond Crystal; Use half for table salt) (for sprinkling over veggies)

3 slices **black forest ham** (skip for vegetarian/vegan)

2 tsp **toasted white sesame seeds**

DRESSING
3 Tbsp **rice vinegar**

2 ½ Tbsp **soy sauce** (use GF soy sauce for GF)

1 Tbsp **sugar**

1 Tbsp **sesame oil** (roasted)

Instructions

1. Follow the packaging instructions to rehydrate harusame (about 4 minutes). Rinse under cold water to remove the starch. Drain well so the dressing won't be diluted. Cut into shorter lengths if you like.
2. Rehydrate wakame in water for 15 minutes. Squeeze the water out and set aside.
3. Cut the cucumber in half lengthwise and thinly slice diagonally.
4. Cut carrot into thin slabs and cut into julienne strips.
5. Sprinkle kosher salt over the cucumber and carrot and coat well. Set aside for 5 minutes. Then quickly rinse off the salt and squeeze water out. Set aside.
6. Cut the black forest ham into julienne strips. Now all the ingredients are ready.
7. In a medium bowl, combine the dressing ingredients and whisk all together.
8. In a large bowl, add harusame, vegetables, ham, and sesame seeds, and pour the dressing. Toss all together. Chill the salad in the fridge for at least 30 minutes before serving.

TO STORE
You can keep in the fridge for up to 2 days.

1 Tbsp **neutral-flavored oil**
(vegetable, canola, etc)

kosher/sea salt (I use Diamond
Crystal; Use half for table salt)

freshly ground blackpepper

Spinach Ohitashi (Japanese Spinach Salad)

This method infuses ingredients with umami and subtle flavor but retains the food's natural taste. It's one of common methods we use to prepare vegetable dishes.

 PREP TIME: 15 Minutes   **COOK TIME:** 5 Minutes   4 Servings

Ingredients

1 bunch **spinach**

Pinch **kosher/sea salt** (I use Diamond Crystal; Use half for table salt)

KOMBU DASHI or AWASE DASHI
½ cup **water** (120 ml)

1 **kombu (dried kelp)** (5 g, about 2"x 2" or 5 cm x 5 cm)

SEASONINGS
1 Tbsp **mirin**

1 Tbsp **usukuchi (lightcolor) soy sauce**

TOPPINGS
toasted white sesame seeds (for vegan/ vegetarian)

katsuobushi (dried bonito flakes) (for nonvegan/ vegetarian)

Instructions

TO MAKE KOMBU DASHI
1. In a saucepan, put water and kombu.
2. Slowly bring it to a boil. Once boiling, remove the kombu from the liquid (You can make Kombu Tsukudani with the used kombu). If you are not vegan/vegetarian, you can add a small amount of katsuobushi to make Awase Dashi for more flavors.

TO MAKE SAVORY BROTH
1. In Kombu Dashi, add mirin and usukuchi soy sauce.
2. Mix together and once it boils, turn off the heat.

TO PREPARE SPINACH
1. Rinse the spinach and boil a large pot of water.
2. When the water is boiling, add the salt and put the spinach in the pot from the stem side first because it takes longer to cook. After 15 seconds, you can push down the leafy part into the water and cook for 1 minute. (US spinach is more tender than Japanese spinach, so it cooks faster).
3. Once the spinach is cooked through, take it out quickly.
4. Transfer spinach to iced water and let it cool (but don't leave the spinach in the ice water too long as you will lose the nutrients).
5. As soon as it's cooled, collect spinach and squeeze water out. Optional, but you can separate the stems and the leafy greens for presentation purpose.
6. Cut the spinach into 1 ½ inch lengths and squeeze the water out one more time.
7. Put the spinach in an airtight container and pour the sauce over.
8. Make sure the spinach is evenly distributed in the container and soak in the sauce. Put the lid on and let it soak in the refrigerator for at least 1 hour (3-4 hours ideally).

TO SERVE

1. Serve the spinach in a bowl and pour the sauce over. I like to make sure each bowl gets both the stems and the leafy greens. The contrasting colors make the dish pop.
2. Sprinkle sesame seeds for vegan/vegetarian version, and bonito-flakes for non-vegan/vegetarian version.

TO STORE

You can keep in the refrigerator for up to 3 days.

Eggplant Agebitashi

Do you adore eggplant? This Eggplant Agebitashi could be your new favorite. The long, slender Japanese eggplant is first deep-fried until crispy brown, then soaked in flavorful dashi and soy sauce-based broth.

 PREP TIME: 15 Minutes   **COOK TIME:** 15 Minutes   4 Servings

Ingredients

2 **Japanese** (or 1 **Chinese eggplant**)

2 cups **neutral-flavored oil** (vegetable, canola, etc) (480 ml) (for deep frying)

3 inch **daikon radish** (7.5 cm) (green top part for sweet taste)

1 **green onion/scallion**

1 knob **ginger** (1 inch, 2.5 cm)

⅓ cup **katsuobushi (dried bonito flakes)** (3 g)

SAUCE
¾ cup **dashi** (Japanese soup stock) (180 ml)

3 Tbsp **mirin** (45 ml)

3 Tbsp **sake** (45 ml)

3 Tbsp **gluten-free soy sauce** (45 ml) (can be regular soy sauce)

1 heaping Tbsp **sugar**

Instructions

1. In a saucepan, combine the sauce ingredients and mix it all together. Bring it to a boil and turn off the heat (keep it covered so the sauce doesn't evaporate).
2. In a deep frying pot/saucepan, add the deep-frying oil and bring to 320°F (160°C).
3. Check if the oil has reached at 320°F (160°C) by putting the wooden chopsticks into the oil. If you see the small bubbles coming from the chopsticks, the oil is ready.
4. While waiting for the oil, we prepare the eggplant. Usually eggplant is soaked in water to prevent discoloration. For this recipe, however, we will skip this process to prevent the oil from contacting with water. Therefore, you will cut the eggplant right before deep frying to avoid discoloration. Discard the tops of the eggplant and cut in half lengthwise.
5. Make incisions on the eggplant diagonally (or cut in a crisscross pattern). Do not cut through, and the intervals should be ⅛ inch (2-3 mm).
6. Cut each eggplant into 3-4 sections. Make sure to wipe off any moisture with paper towel.
7. Gently put a few pieces of the eggplant into the oil (skin facing down), and deep fry for 2 to 2 ½ minutes. Do not overcrowd the pot as the oil temperature will drop too fast and the eggplant will get mushy and greasy. If the oil temperature is too low, take out the eggplant and wait till the oil reaches the right temperature. Once the eggplants are cooked, remove from the oil and drain on a wire rack, skin facing up. Deep fry the next batch, until all the eggplant pieces are deep-fried.

8. When the eggplants are cooled, transfer to a rimmed container or dish. Heat up the sauce until hot and then pour the hot sauce over to soak the eggplant for several hours (at least 1 hour). If you want to serve this dish chilled, put it in the refrigerator.
9. While soaking, peel the daikon and grate.
10. Cut green onion and grate ginger.

TO SERVE

Place the eggplant in a serving dish and sprinkle some katsuobushi. Put grated daikon and grated ginger on top. Pour the sauce over and garnish with green onion. Serve chilled or at room temperature.

TO STORE

You can keep it in the refrigerator up to 2-3 days.

Green Bean Shiraae (Mashed Tofu Salad)

Shiraae or Mashed Tofu Salad is a classic Japanese dish made of tender green beans, creamy tofu, sesame seeds, and savory miso. This vegan-friendly salad is super easy to make and can be on your dinner table in no time!

 PREP TIME: 5 Minutes   **COOK TIME:** 5 Minutes   2 Servings

Ingredients

7 oz **silken/soft tofu** (200 g)

9 oz **green beans** (250 g)

SEASONINGS
4 Tbsp **toasted white sesame seeds** (30 g)

1 Tbsp **sugar**

2 tsp **miso** (I use Hikari Miso® Organic White Miso)

1 tsp **soy sauce**

⅛ tsp **kosher/ sea salt** (I use Diamond Crystal; Use half for table salt)

Instructions

TO PREPARE TOFU
1. Do not skip this step. You don't want to drain the water from tofu completely, but it's important to remove some moisture so the dressing doesn't get too wet. Wrap the tofu with paper towels.
2. Put the wrapped tofu on a tray or plate. Add another tray or plate on top of the tofu and put a heavy object on top to facilitate draining. Set aside for 30 minutes.

TO PREPARE GREEN BEANS
1. Bring a big pot of water to a boil. Tear off the ends of green beans.
2. Boil green beans until crisp-tender.
3. Drain well and set aside.
4. Cut the green beans diagonally into 2-inch pieces.
5. Pour the soy sauce and toss together. Set aside for later.

TO PREPARE SESAME SEEDS
1. Toast the sesame seeds in a frying pan, shaking the pan frequently, until they are fragrant and start to pop. Transfer to a Japanese mortar (Suribachi).
2. Grind sesame seeds in the Japanese mortar (suribachi) with a pestle (surikogi).

TO MAKE TOFU DRESSING
1. Add sugar and miso.
2. Mix well until sugar and miso are incorporated into the ground sesame seeds.
3. Remove tofu from the paper towel. Break it into pieces with your hands and add to the sesame seed mixture.
4. Using a pestle, mash and grind the tofu until smooth or to your liking.

5. Season the tofu with salt and have a taste. It should not be bland. Green beans will be added, so the tofu dressing should have good flavor at this stage.
6. Mix all together until smooth.

TO ASSEMBLE

1. Shake off any excess soy sauce from the green beans first. Any liquid from the soy sauce will dilute the dressing. Then add the seasoned green beans to the tofu dressing. Combine well.
2. Once combined, you can chill in the refrigerator for 30 minutes before serving, or serve immediately.

TO STORE

1. You can keep it for 24 hours in the refrigerator; however, I recommend consuming it soon.
2. To store any leftover tofu, keep it in an airtight container and pour water until it covers the tofu. Keep in the refrigerator (change the water every day) and use it within a few days.

Carrot Ginger Dressing

Love the Carrot Ginger Dressing served at Japanese restaurants? Made with carrot, ginger, and miso, this sweet-tangy dressing will zest up your salad!

 PREP TIME: 10 Minutes   6 Servings (roughly 1 ½ cup)

Ingredients

1 **carrot** (4.8 oz, 135 g)

¼ **onion** (2.5 oz, 70 g)

1 knob **ginger** (1 inch, 2.5 cm) preferably young/spring ginger for a milder taste)

1 ½ Tbsp **sugar**

1 Tbsp **miso** (I use mild and mellow white miso)

¼ tsp **kosher/sea salt** (I use Diamond Crystal; Use half for table salt) (to taste)

freshly ground black pepper (to taste)

1 tsp **sesame oil** (roasted)

½ cup **rice vinegar** (120 ml)

¼ cup **neutral-flavored oil** (vegetable, canola, etc) (60 ml)

Instructions

1. Peel the carrot and chop it into ½ to 1 inch pieces.
2. Chop onion into 1-inch pieces.
3. Peel the ginger and slice into small pieces. Put all the chopped vegetables into the food processor.
4. Puree the veggies until fine and smooth.
5. Add sugar, miso, salt, and pepper.
6. Add sesame oil, rice vinegar, and oil.
7. Process until the dressing is completely smooth. Taste the dressing and adjust with salt. If it's too sour, add a bit more sugar. If you prefer the dressing to be lighter, add water to thin it (I don't add water so the dressing will last longer).

TO SERVE AND STORE

Shake well before you serve over a green salad (here I used iceberg lettuce, cucumber slices, and tomatoes). You can store the dressing in an airtight container like a mason jar for up to 1 week after using. If you take out the portion you need and put the dressing back into the refrigerator right away, you can keep it for up to 2 weeks.

Japanese Kani Salad

This healthy and flavorful Japanese Kani Salad is so easy to whip up, and it's absolutely amazing when tossed in a light and refreshing ponzu mayonnaise dressing! It's guaranteed to be a hit with your entire family!

 PREP TIME: 20 Minutes   2 Servings

Ingredients

5 oz **imitation crab meat (kanikama)** (142 g; I used 1 package of Japanese brand of kanikama)

½ **English cucumber** (6 oz, 170 g)

½ cup **corn kernels** (3 oz, 85 g; canned or frozen, frozen corn can just be run under cold water to defrost, drain, and then it's ready to use.)

PONZU MAYONNAISE DRESSING:
2 Tbsp **Japanese mayonnaise**

1 Tbsp **ponzu** (Or use my Homemade Ponzu recipe)

1 Tbsp **toasted white sesame seeds**

½ tsp **soy sauce**

Instructions

1. Cut the imitation crab in half (if necessary) and shred it. Peel the English cucumber with a stripe pattern. Cut the cucumber in half lengthwise and cut diagonally into thin slices.
2. In a medium bowl, combine shredded imitation crab, cucumber slices, and corn. Add the dressing ingredients to the bowl and combine well. Serve the salad in individual bowls or a large serving bowl. Enjoy!

IF YOU MAKE THE SALAD AHEAD OF TIME:
Keep the ingredients and the dressing separately in the refrigerator. Mix together right before you serve.

Ramen Egg

Ramen Eggs (Ajitsuke Tamago) are delicious as topping on ramen or enjoyed as a snack. Read on to learn how to make this flavorful soft boiled eggs recipe at home.

 PREP TIME: 10 Minutes   **COOK TIME:** 10 Minutes   2 Eggs

Ingredients

2 **large eggs** (50 g each w/o shell) (refrigerated till Step 3; You can use up to 4 eggs with this recipe)

SEASONINGS
2 Tbsp **soy sauce**

2 Tbsp **mirin**

3-6 Tbsp **water** (Read my tip in the instructions)

Instructions

1. In a resealable plastic bag, combine soy sauce, mirin, and water. *Tip 1: If you plan to make the ramen eggs in just a few hours of marinating, use 0-1 Tbsp water. Otherwise, start with 2-3 Tbsp water and taste before adding more water. Adjust the saltiness to your taste and how long you plan to marinade. Tip 2: To use the minimal amount of the condiments, I use a plastic bag. If you use a container, you will need to double the amount of condiment to cover the eggs.*

2. Bring water to a boil in a medium saucepan. There should be enough water to cover the eggs (should be 1 inch above the eggs).

3. When boiling, carefully and slowly submerge the eggs into the boiling water with a mesh strainer or ladle to prevent the eggs from cracking.

4. Immediately reduce the heat to maintain a simmer (gentle boil) and cook the eggs for exactly 7 minutes. Make sure the water is simmering, but not so hot that the eggs bounce around. If you want your egg yolk to be in the center, gently rotate the eggs with chopsticks once in a while for the first 3 minutes so the egg yolk will be in the center.

5. After 7 minutes, immediately take out the eggs and soak in the ice bath to stop them from cooking further. Let cool for 3 minutes.

6. The soft boiled eggs are not completely hardened so gently peel the eggs.

7. Put the peeled eggs in the sauce bag and close tightly. They should be submerged in the marinade. Marinate overnight to up to 3-4 days in the refrigerator.

8. Take out the eggs and cut in halves to serve. Enjoy the eggs by themselves or use them as a ramen topping. *Tip: Increase the marinate ingredients if you cook more than 4 eggs.*

TO STORE

Keep the eggs in the refrigerator all the time. Enjoy within 4 days if your eggs are soft-boiled. If your eggs are hard-boiled, you can keep in the refrigerator for up to a week. For food safety, I recommend discarding the marinade and making a new batch if you want to make more.

Tamagoyaki (Japanese Rolled Omelette)

Sweet yet savory, Tamagoyaki (Japanese rolled omelette), makes a delightful Japanese breakfast or side dish for your bento lunches.

 PREP TIME: 5 Minutes   **COOK TIME:** 5 Minutes   2 Servings

Ingredients

3 **large eggs** (50 g each w/o shell)

2 Tbsp **neutral-flavored oil** (vegetable, canola, etc)

1 ½ sheet **nori (seaweed)** (optional; for omelette with nori in it)

SEASONINGS
3 Tbsp **dashi** (Japanese soup stock) (use Kombu Dashi for vegetarian) (45 ml)

2 tsp **sugar**

1 tsp **soy sauce** (use GF soy sauce for gluten-free)

1 tsp **mirin**

2 pinch **kosher/sea salt** (I use Diamond Crystal; use half for table salt)

GARNISH
3 oz **daikon radish** (1", 2.5 cm; choose green top part as it

Instructions

1. Gently whisk the eggs in a bowl. It's best to "cut" the eggs with chopsticks in a zig-zag motion and do not over mix.
2. In another bowl, combine the seasonings and mix well.
3. Pour the seasoning mixture into the eggs mixture and whisk gently. Then pour the mixture into a measuring cup with spout and handle (it'll be easier to pour into the frying pan).

TAMAGOYAKI PAN METHOD
1. Heat the pan over medium heat, dip a folded paper towel in oil and apply to the pan. Put a little bit of egg mixture to see if the pan is hot.
2. When you hear the sizzling sound, pour a thin layer of egg mixture in the pan, tilting to cover the bottom of the pan.
3. Poke the air bubbles to release the air. After the bottom of the egg has set but is still soft on top, start rolling into a log shape from one side to the other.
4. Move the rolled omelette to the side where you started to roll, and apply oil to the pan with a paper towel, even under the omelette.
5. Pour the egg mixture to cover the bottom of the pan again. Make sure to lift the omelette to spread the mixture underneath.
6. When the new layer of egg has set and is still soft on top, start rolling from one side to the other.
7. Repeat the process one more time. Move the rolled omelette to the side where you started to roll, and apply oil to the pan with a paper towel, even under the omelette.
8. Pour the egg mixture to cover the bottom of the pan again. Make sure to lift the omelette to spread the mixture under-

is sweeter than white part) (85 g)

soy sauce (use GF soy sauce for gluten-free)

neath.

9. Remove from the pan and place the omelette on the bamboo sushi mat and wrap it up. Shape the egg when it is still hot. Let it stand for 5 minutes.

TO SERVE

1. Slice the omelette into ½" (1 cm) pieces.
2. Peel and grate daikon. Gently squeeze water out. Serve Tamagoyaki with grated daikon and pour soy sauce over daikon.

TO KEEP

You can put tamagoyaki in an airtight container and store in the freezer for up to 2 weeks. Defrost overnight in the refrigerator or microwave.

MAIN DISHES

Ginger Pork (Shogayaki)

Classic Japanese ginger pork recipe. One of my favorite homemade dishes with tender sliced pork loin in sweet ginger sauce. Ready in 20 minutes!

 PREP TIME: 10 Minutes   **COOK TIME:** 10 Minutes   2 Servings

Ingredients

½ lb **thinly sliced pork loin** (I use sukiyaki meat)(227 g)

¼ **onion**

1 clove **garlic**

1 knob **ginger** (about 1 tsp.)

kosher/sea salt (I use Diamond Crystal; Use half for table salt)

freshly ground black pepper

1 Tbsp **neutral-flavored oil** (vegetable, canola, etc)

1 green onion/scallion (finely chopped)

SEASONINGS
2 Tbsp **soy sauce**

2 Tbsp **mirin**

2 Tbsp **sake**

1 tsp **sugar**

Instructions

1. In a small bowl, grate onion, garlic, and ginger.
2. Add the seasonings. We like our ginger pork to be a little bit sweeter, so we add 1 tsp. sugar (optional you can skip the sugar).
3. Season the meat with salt and pepper.
4. In a large non-stick frying pan, heat oil on medium-high. Put the meat in a single layer (cook in batches). Flip the meat when the bottom side is golden brown. If the meat is thin, cook time will be short. Make sure you don't overcook the pork or else it gets tough (but also be careful not to under-cook).
5. When the meat is cooked through, add the seasonings and chopped scallion. Serve immediately.

Japanese Croquettes (Korokke)

Soft creamy potato with ground meat inside a tasty crunchy shell, Japanese Croquettes or Korokke is my favorite Japanese food. This is my mother's recipe.

 PREP TIME: 30 Minutes   **COOK TIME:** 1 Hour   16 Croquettes

Ingredients

FOR POTATO AND MEAT MIXTURE

2 lb **russet potatoes** (900 g, about 4 potatoes; please use Russet potatoes)

1 **onion** (9.6 oz, 272 g)

1 Tbsp **neutral-flavored oil** (vegetable, canola, etc)

1 lb **ground beef** (454 g; 85% lean)

½ tsp **kosher/sea salt** (I use Diamond Crystal; Use half for table salt) (for meat)

¼ tsp **freshly ground black pepper** (for meat)

1 Tbsp **unsalted butter** (for potato)

½ tsp **kosher/sea salt** (I use Diamond Crystal; Use half for table salt) (for potatoes)

¼ tsp **freshly ground black pepper** (for potatoes)

Instructions

TO MAKE POTATO AND MEAT MIXTURE

1. Wash the potatoes under cold running water. Peel the potatoes and remove the eyes.
2. Cut each potato into equal 4 pieces. Tip: To cook evenly, it's important that they are in a similar size.
3. In a large pot, put water and potatoes and bring it to a boil covered on medium heat, leaving the lid slightly ajar to prevent from boiling over. It will take about 15 minutes to boil. Cook potatoes until a skewer goes through the potato easily, about 15-20 minutes.
4. While the potatoes are cooking, chop the onion into ¼ inch pieces. If the onions need to be chopped finer, you can run your knife through them in a rocking motion.
5. In a large skillet, heat oil on medium heat and add the chopped onion.
6. Sauté the onion until translucent and tender, about 12-15 minutes. *Tip: Make sure there is no moisture left so that the croquette doesn't get soggy. Leave the chopped onions for a long stretch between stirring to give them nice char. Careful not to burn.*
7. Add the meat and break it up with a wooden spoon.
8. Season the mixture with salt and black pepper.
9. Stir to combine, turn off the heat when the meat is no longer pink. Remove from heat to let cool slightly.
10. Once in a while, you have to check if the potatoes are done cooking. Insert a skewer to a bigger piece of the potatoes and if it goes through easily, it's done. Remove the potatoes from the heat and drain the water completely. *Tip: Use a lid to cover so the potatoes don't fall out from the pot.*
11. Move the pot back to the stove. Shake the pot over low heat

FOR PANKO COATING
½ cup **all-purpose flour** (plain flour) (60 g)

3 **large eggs** (50 g each w/o shell)

2 cups **panko (Japanese breadcrumbs)** (120 g)

FOR DEEP FRYING
4 cups **neutral-flavored oil** (vegetable, canola, etc) (946 ml; for deep frying)

TO SERVE
Tonkatsu Sauce

and let the remaining moisture completely evaporate (but don't burn the potatoes), about 2-3 minutes. Then transfer to a large bowl.

12. With a potato masher, mash the potatoes while they are still hot and let the steam escape. Add the butter. *Tip: keep some potato chunks for texture.* Add salt and pepper and combine well together.

13. To avoid adding excess cooking liquid from the meat mixture to the mashed potatoes, gently squeeze the liquid out from the mixture by collecting it to one side of the pan.

14. Add the meat mixture into the mashed potatoes in the bowl and combine together.

15. While the mixture is still warm, but not hot, start making the patties (traditionally, oval shape, roughly 3-inch in length), avoiding air pockets.

16. Cover and let the Korokke patties rest in the fridge for 15-30 minutes (Do not skip!). *Tip: Resting and cooling down the patties prevents the croquettes from exploding while deep frying. The cold patties in the hot oil will not release any steam. If patties are still warm, the temperature of the patties will go up and start to steam, which will then puncture a hole in the panko coating and explode.*

17. Prepare a tray each for flour and panko, and crack eggs into a small bowl and whisk to combine..

18. Coat each patty in flour and shake off excess.

19. Then dredge in the whisked egg and coat with panko.

20. Once you finish coating the patties, add the oil to a medium pot. Make sure there are at least 2 inches (5 cm) of oil in the pot so the entire croquette will be covered.

21. Bring the oil to 340-350°F (171-178°C) over medium heat. Use a cooking thermometer to check the oil temperature (no guessing!).

22. Deep fry 2-3 croquettes at a time until they are golden brown, about 2-3 minutes. *Tip: Do not touch the croquettes until one side is golden brown. The inside is already cooked, so all you need to do is to fry until golden brown!*

23. Transfer the croquettes to a wire rack or paper towel to drain the excess oil.

TO SERVE
Serve the croquettes with Tonkatsu sauce. Typically, deep fried foods are served with shredded cabbage in Japan.

TO STORE

You can store the leftovers in an airtight container and freeze up to a month. To reheat, put the defrosted or frozen croquettes on a baking sheet lined with aluminum foil or parchment paper. Bake at 350°F (180°C) for 15-20 minutes for defrosted ones or 45 minutes for frozen ones. Check if the inside is warm before serving.

Baked Tonkatsu

Crispy on the outside and juicy on the inside, this Baked Tonkatsu recipe is a total game changer. All you need is the right techniques and tips to achieve the perfection. Serve with tonkatsu sauce, you can now enjoy this popular dish at home.

 PREP TIME: 10 Minutes   **COOK TIME:** 20 Minutes   2 Servings

Ingredients

¾ cup **panko (Japanese breadcrumbs)** 45 g

1 Tbsp **extra-virgin olive oil**

2 **boneless pork loin chops** (½ inch thick) (½ lb or 227 g, ½" = 1.2 cm)

1 tsp **kosher/sea salt** (I use Diamond Crystal; Use half for table salt)

freshly ground black pepper

2 Tbsp **all-purpose flour** (plain flour)(15 g)

1 **large egg** (50 g w/o shell)

Tonkatsu Sauce

1 Tbsp **toasted white and black sesame seed**

Instructions

Adjust an oven rack to the middle position and preheat the oven to 400 °F (200 °C). Put a wire rack on a rimmed baking sheet or line with parchment paper.

TO PRE-TOAST PANKO
Combine the panko and oil in a frying pan and toast over medium heat until golden brown. Transfer panko into a shallow dish and allow to cool.

TO PREPARE THE PORK
1. Get rid of the extra fat and make a couple of slits on the connective tissue between the meat and fat. The reason why you do this is that red meat and fat have different elasticity, and when they are cooked they will shrink and expand at different rates. This will allow Tonkatsu to stay nice and flat and prevent it from curling up.
2. Pound both sides of the meat with a meat pounder, or if you don't have one then just use the back of the knife to pound. Mold the extended meat back into the original shape with your hands.
3. Sprinkle salt and freshly ground black pepper.
4. Dredge each pork piece in the flour to coat completely and pat off the excess flour. Then dip into the beaten egg and finally coat with the toasted panko. Press on the panko flakes to make sure they adhere to the pork.

TO BAKE
1. Place the pork on the prepared baking sheet or even better if you have an oven-safe wire rack (as air goes through on the bottom so panko won't get crushed). Bake at 400°F (200°C) until the pork is no longer pink inside, about 20 minutes.

2. Cut Tonkatsu into 1 inch pieces (so you can eat with chopsticks) by pressing the knife directly down instead of moving back and forth. This way the panko will not come off. Transfer to a plate and serve immediately.

3. To make special sesame tonkatsu sauce, grind black and white sesame seeds in a mortar and add tonkatsu sauce. Mix all together.

TO STORE

You can freeze the fried and cooled baked katsu in an airtight container or freezer bag for up to a month. To reheat, bake it at 375°F (190°C) on a wire rack until the inside is warm.

Teriyaki Salmon

Quick and easy teriyaki salmon recipe. Salmon fillet is pan-grilled until tender perfection in an authentic Japanese homemade teriyaki sauce.

 PREP TIME: 5 Minutes   **COOK TIME:** 10 Minutes   2 Servings

Ingredients

2 **fillets salmon with skin** (2 fillets = ½ to ¾ lb, 227-340 g) (½ to ¾", 1.3-2 cm thickness, skin will hold the flesh together while cooking)

¼ tsp **kosher/sea salt** (I use Diamond Crystal; Use half for table salt)

⅛ tsp **freshly ground black pepper**

1 Tbsp **all-purpose flour** (plain flour) (7.5 g)

½ Tbsp **neutral-flavored oil** (vegetable, canola, etc)

1 Tbsp **unsalted butter**

1 Tbsp **sake** (or Chinese rice wine or dry sherry)

SEASONINGS
1 Tbsp **sake** (or Chinese rice wine or dry sherry)

1 Tbsp **mirin** (or 1 Tbsp. sake + 1 tsp. sugar)

1 Tbsp **sugar**

2 Tbsp **soy sauce**

Instructions

1. Combine the ingredients for seasonings and mix well until the sugar is mostly dissolved (or you can microwave it for a few seconds). Rinse the salmon and pat dry. Season the salmon with kosher salt and black pepper on both sides.
2. Sprinkle ½ Tbsp of all-purpose flour on one side of salmon and spread evenly. Flip over and sprinkle the rest of flour on the other side. Gently remove the excess flour.
3. In a frying pan, add the vegetable oil and melt the butter over medium heat. Don't burn the butter. If the frying pan gets too hot, reduce heat or remove from the heat temporarily.
4. Add the salmon fillets, skin side on the bottom. Cook the salmon for 3 minutes, or until the bottom side is nicely browned, and then flip.
5. Add sake and cover with lid. Steam the salmon for 3 minutes, or until it's cooked through. Remove the salmon to a plate.
6. Add the seasonings to the pan and increase the heat a slightly. When the sauce starts to boil, add salmon back in the pan and spoon the sauce over the salmon.
7. When the sauce thickens, turn off the heat. Plate the salmon on a plate and serve immediately.

Karaage (Japanese Fried Chicken)

Let's make Karaage (Japanese fried chicken), one of the greatest fried chickens in the world! It's exceptionally flavorful, juicy and ultra crispy.

 PREP TIME: 15 Minutes   **COOK TIME:** 15 Minutes   4 Servings

Ingredients

1.5 lb **boneless, skin-on chicken thighs** (680 g or 4- 6 pieces; Read the blog post)

½ tsp **kosher/sea salt** (I use Diamond Crystal; Use half for table salt)

freshly ground black pepper

2 Tbsp **potato starch/ cornstarch** (Add more if necessary; Read blog post)

2 Tbsp **all-purpose flour** (plain flour) (Add more if necessary) (15 g)

4 cups **neutral-flavored oil** (vegetable, canola, etc) (for deep frying) (960 ml)

SEASONINGS
1 knob **ginger** (You'll only need ½ tsp grated ginger)

1 clove **garlic**

Instructions

1. Cut each chicken thigh into 2-inch pieces and season with salt and freshly ground black pepper.
2. Grate the ginger (you will only need ½ tsp) and mince the garlic (I usually use a garlic presser).
3. In a large bowl, combine ginger, garlic, ½ Tbsp soy sauce, ½ Tbsp sake, and ½ tsp sesame oil. Whisk all together.
4. Add the chicken to the bowl and mix with your hands. Cover and keep in the refrigerator to marinate for 30 minutes.
5. Pour the oil in a heavy-bottomed pot, bring the oil to 325 °F (163 °C) over medium heat.
6. Meanwhile, prepare potato starch and all-purpose flour in separate bowls.
7. First, lightly dredge each chicken piece in the flour and dust off the excess. Then dredge the chicken in the potato starch and remove the excess. Continue with the remaining chicken.
8. When the oil temperature has reached 325 °F (163 °C) (insert a wooden chopstick in the oil and see if small bubbles appear around it), gently submerge each chicken piece into the oil. Do not overcrowd; add 3-5 pieces at a time. If you put many pieces in the oil, the oil temperature will drop quickly and chicken will end up absorbing too much oil.
9. **First Deep Frying:** Deep fry for 90 seconds, or until the outside of the chicken is a light golden color. If the chicken changes color too quickly, then the oil temperature is too high. Either put a few more pieces of chicken in the oil or lower the heat. Controlling oil temperature at all times is very important for deep frying. Transfer to a wire rack to drain excess oil.
10. The chicken will continue to cook with the remaining heat on the wire rack. Continue with the remaining chicken. Between batches, pick up crumbs in the oil with a fine-mesh sieve. This

½ Tbsp **soy sauce**

½ Tbsp **sake** (Sub: dry sherry or Chinese rice wine or skip)

½ tsp **sesame oil** (roasted)

GARNISH (OPTIONAL)
Lemon (for taste and garnish)

Japanese mayonnaise (optional for dipping)

shichimi togarashi (Japanese seven spice) (optional for spicy taste)

keeps the oil clean and prevents it from becoming too dark.

11. **2nd Deep Frying:** Now heat the oil to 350°F (177°C). Deep fry for 45 seconds, or until the skin is nice golden color and crispy. Transfer to a wire rack to drain excess oil and continue with the remaining chicken.

TO SERVE AND STORE

1. Serve the chicken hot. Karaage is often served with a wedge of lemon and Japanese mayo (sprinkle shichimi togarashi for a bit of spice). To store, deep fry all the chicken, let cool completely, and keep in an airtight container. You can store in the refrigerator for up to 3 days and in the freezer for up to a month.

Grilled Mackerel (Saba Shioyaki)

Baked in the oven, this Grilled Mackerel or Saba Shioyaki is the simplest fish recipe you can make on your busy weeknight. Serve with steamed rice, miso soup, and salad for a wholesome meal.

 PREP TIME: 5 Minutes   **COOK TIME:** 20 Minutes   2 Servings

Ingredients

10 oz **mackerel** (saba) (280 g, 2 fillets)

2 Tbsp **sake**

½ tsp **kosher/sea salt** (I use Diamond Crystal; Use half for table salt)

1 inch **daikon radish** (grated, to serve)

1 tsp **soy sauce** (to serve)

1 wedge **lemon**

Instructions

1. Coat the fish with 2 Tbsp sake.
2. Pat dry with paper towel (discard the sake) and transfer the fish to a baking sheet lined with parchment paper.
3. Sprinkle ½ tsp salt on both sides of the fish.
4. Let it sit at room temperature for 20 minutes. Preheat the oven to 400°F (200°C) with a rack placed in the middle.
5. After 20 minutes, pat dry the excess moisture from the fish.
6. Place the fish skin side down and bake for 15-20 minutes, or until the flesh is golden brown.
7. Grate daikon radish if using.
8. Serve the grilled mackerel with grated daikon and a lemon wedge on the side. Pour a few drops of soy sauce on grated daikon to eat with the fish. Enjoy!

Mapo Tofu

The Japanese-style Mapo Tofu (Mabo Dofu) is incredibly flavorful but less spicy than the Sichuan-style. A delicious meal ready in 30 minutes that even children can enjoy!

 PREP TIME: 10 Minutes   **COOK TIME:** 15 Minutes   4 Servings

Ingredients

2 cloves **garlic**

1 knob **ginger** (1 inch, 2.5 cm)

2 **green onions/scallions**

14 oz **silken/soft tofu** (396 g)

1 Tbsp **neutral-flavored oil** (vegetable, canola, etc)

½ lb **ground pork** (227 g; or any other meat/veggies of your choice)

SEASONINGS
2 ½ Tbsp **Doubanjiang (spicy chili bean sauce/broad bean paste)** I use 1 ½ Tbsp Doubanjiang (non-spicy) and 1 Tbsp Ladoubanjigang (spicy).
2 Tbsp **mirin**

1 Tbsp **miso**

1 Tbsp **oyster sauce**

½ Tbsp **soy sauce**

1 tsp **sesame oil** (roasted)

1 tsp **potato starch/cornstarch**

4 Tbsp **water**

Instructions

1. Combine all the ingredients for the seasonings in a bowl and mix well together.
2. Mince the garlic cloves and ginger.
3. Cut the green onions into small pieces. Drain the tofu and cut into about 1 inch (2.5 cm) cubes.
4. In a large frying pan, heat vegetable oil on medium heat and sauté garlic and ginger. Make sure you don't burn them. Once they are fragrant, add the ground pork and break it up with a spatula or wooden spoon.
5. When the meat is no longer pink, add the Seasoning mixture and stir thoroughly.
6. Bring the sauce to a boil, then add in tofu and gently mix everything together. Stir frequently, without mashing up the tofu, until it is heated through. Add the green onions and mix just before taking the pan off the heat. Serve immediately.

Stir Fry Vegetables (Yasai Itame)

Cooking a healthy meal for your family on busy weeknight is made possible with this Stir fry Vegetables (Yasai Itame). Loaded with plenty of vegetables and your choice of protein, everything comes together in less than 30 minutes!

 PREP TIME: 5 Minutes   **COOK TIME:** 10 Minutes   4 Servings

Ingredients

6.5 oz **thinly sliced pork** (185 g; skip for vegetarian/vegan)

10 **snow peas** (about 1 oz, 30 g)

¼ **onion** (about 3 oz, 90 g)

¼ **cabbage** (about 7 oz, 200 g)

½ **carrot** (about 3 oz, 90 g)

1 clove **garlic**

1 knob **ginger** (1 inch, 2.5 cm)

1 Tbsp **neutral-flavored oil** (vegetable, canola, etc)

2 cups **bean sprouts** (about 3.5 oz, 100 g; loosely packed)

FOR PORK MARINADE
1 tsp **soy sauce**

1 tsp **sake**

FOR SEASONINGS
1 tsp **oyster sauce** (for

Instructions

1. Cut the meat into smaller pieces if necessary, and marinate the meat with 1 tsp soy sauce and 1 tsp sake in a small bowl.
2. Remove the strings from snow peas and cut the onion into thin slices.
3. Cut the cabbage into 1" (2.5 cm) pieces.
4. Cut the carrot into 2" (5 cm) long slabs then cut into matchsticks.
5. Crush (or mince) the garlic and mince the ginger.
6. In a large frying pan or wok, heat 1 Tbsp vegetable oil on medium-high. Once it's hot, add the garlic and ginger. When fragrant, add the meat and cook until it's about 80% done. Alternatively, you can cook until no longer pink and take the meat out, then add the meat back in when all the veggies are cooked. This will prevent the meat from getting overcooked.
7. Add the onion and stir fry until almost tender. Then add the carrot. If you are going to add other kinds of vegetables that are not in the recipe, start cooking the thicker and tougher vegetables first as they take a longer time to cook.
8. Once the carrot is getting tender, add the cabbage and snow peas. Continue to stir and toss the ingredients.
9. Then add the bean sprouts and toss one more time. Add 1 tsp. oyster sauce and 1 tsp. soy sauce.
10. Add the salt, freshly ground black pepper, and drizzle 2 tsp. sesame oil. Enjoy immediately; this dish is fantastic with rice and miso soup.

vegetarian/vegan, use vegetarian oyster sauce or skip)

1 tsp **soy sauce** (for gluten-free, use GF soy sauce)

½ tsp **kosher/sea salt** (I use Diamond Crystal; Use half for table salt)

freshly ground black pepper

2 tsp **sesame oil** (roasted)

Menchi Katsu (Ground Meat Cutlet)

Breaded in panko breadcrumbs and deep fried to golden color, these Menchi Katsu (Japanese Ground Meat Cutlet) are one of the popular yoshoku foods (western style Japanese food) in Japan.

 PREP TIME: 30 Minutes   **COOK TIME:** 30 Minutes

Ingredients

½ **onion**

1 Tbsp **extra-virgin olive oil**

1 lb **ground beef & pork combination** (normally 70% beef & 30% pork) (454 g)

2 Tbsp **panko** (Japanese breadcrumbs)

1 Tbsp **milk**

1 **large egg** (50 g w/o shell)

½ tsp **nutmeg**

½ tsp **kosher/sea salt** (I use Diamond Crystal; Use half for table salt)

freshly ground black pepper

3 cups **neutral-flavored oil** (vegetable, canola, etc) (700 ml)

FOR COATING PATTIES:
½ cup **all-purpose flour** (plain flour) (for dredging) (60 g)

Instructions

1. Mince the onion and heat the olive oil in a frying pan over medium heat and sauté onion until translucent and golden brown.
2. Transfer the onion to a large bowl and set aside to cool.
3. In the large bowl with the onion, add the ground meat, 2 Tbsp panko, 1 Tbsp milk, 1 large egg, ½ tsp nutmeg, ½ tsp Kosher salt, and freshly ground black pepper.
4. Knead well with hands until the meat mixture becomes pale and sticky.
5. Roughly divide the mixture into 6 balls.
6. Toss each ball from one hand to the other hand repeatedly about 5 times. This helps to release air the inside the balls so the meat patty won't break when you deep fry.
7. Now shape each ball into an oval-shaped patty and place on a plate. Cover with plastic and rest in the refrigerator for 30-60 minutes to solidify the fat.
8. Prepare 3 separate bowls: flour, beaten eggs, and panko. Dredge and coat each patty in flour, egg, and panko.
9. When you coat the patties with panko, fix them into nice oval shape.
10. Heat the oil to 340°F (170°C) and gently place the patties into the oil. Do not crowd the oil as meat patties will decrease the oil temperature too fast.
11. Deep fry for 3 minutes on each side (total 6 minutes). For the first 2 minutes, don't touch the patties as they are soft and easy to break.

2 **large eggs** (50 g each w/o shell) (for dredging)

1 ½ **cup panko (Japanese breadcrumbs)** (for dredging) (90 g)

SAUCE OPTIONS:
Tonkatsu sauce

Worcestershire sauce

Tonkatsu/Worcestershire sauce + ketchup

tartar sauce

12. Drain oil for 1-2 minutes and the remaining heat will cook inside the patty. Pick up the crumbs in the oil as they darken the oil and stick to the new patties.
13. Serve immediately with tonkatsu sauce, Worcestershire sauce, the combination of the two sauces, or the homemade tartar sauce.

TO STORE
Let Menchi Katsu cool completely and store in an airtight container. You can freeze for up to a month. When you're ready to eat, reheat at 350°F (180°C) in the oven.

Kushikatsu (Kushiage)

A hugely popular Osaka street food, Kushikatsu (Kushiage) are skewered meat and veggies that are breaded with panko and deep fried to golden crisp. Dip in a savory sauce to enjoy!

 PREP TIME: 30 Minutes   **COOK TIME:** 25 Minutes   4 Servings

Ingredients

2 cup **panko (Japanese breadcrumbs)** (120 g)

kosher/sea salt (I use Diamond Crystal; Use half for table salt)

freshly ground black pepper

3 ½ cup **neutral-flavored oil** (vegetable, canola, etc) (enough for 10-inch cast iron skillet)(840 ml)

KUSHIKATSU SAUCE (MAKES ½ CUP)
4 Tbsp **Worcestershire sauce** (usuta sauce)

2 Tbsp **ketchup**

2 Tbsp **water** (30 ml)

2 tsp **soy sauce**

2 tsp **sugar**

KUSHIKATSU INGREDIENTS
9 **quail eggs**

Instructions

You will need a pack of 6-inch bamboo skewers for this recipe.

PREPARE INGREDIENTS
1. For Kushikatsu Sauce, combine all the sauce ingredients in a small bowl and whisk well. Depending on the amount of Kushikatsu, multiply the sauce ingredients.
2. Boil the water in a small saucepan, and gently submerge the quail eggs into the boiling water. Cook for 3 minutes and transfer to iced water to let cool. Peel the eggs and set aside.
3. Put panko in the food processor. Run to make the panko into finer texture.
4. Snap the end of asparagus and discard the bottom.
5. Cut ½ onion into 4 wedges.
6. Discard the end of garlic chives and cut them into 4 equal pieces.
7. Cut the pork chop into 4 pieces and pound the meat with the back of the knife to tenderize.
8. Cut the chicken breast diagonally (against the grain) about ½ inch thickness. Then season with kosher salt and freshly ground black pepper.

SKEWER ALL THE INGREDIENTS
1. Skewer the chicken and pork as if you are stitching, starting from one end of the meat, move the skewer downward and upward alternately.
2. Equally divide the garlic chives and put them on each end of the four pork belly slices on the cutting board. Roll the garlic chives from one end to the other. Skewer the seam so the pork belly slice will stay in place.
3. Skewer the sausage and quail eggs.

6 **asparagus**

½ **onion**

1 bunch **garlic chives** about 20 stalks

½ cup **sushi ginger**

2 **sausages**

1 piece **pork loin chop** (½ inch thick)

½ **chicken breast** (butterfly one breast but only use half)

4 slices **pork belly**

KUSHIKATSU BATTER
1 **large egg** (50 g w/o shell)

1 cup **all-purpose flour** (plain flour)(120 g)

¾ to 1 cup **water** (180 to 240 ml)

4. For sushi ginger, drain it and skewer. For onion, skewer it toward the core.
5. Prepare all the skewered ingredients on a plate/tray.

PREPARE BATTER
1. Whisk the egg in a large bowl and add water, leaving about ¼ cup in a measuring cup.
2. Then add the all-purpose flour into the bowl. Whisk all together. Slowly add the rest of water until you reach the right consistency.
3. The batter is runny but thick. When you dip your finger in it, it should cover with the batter. Place the panko in a shallow bowl/tray.

DEEP FRY
1. Bring the oil to 340-360°F (170-180°C). When the oil is hot and ready for deep frying, you want to start with the vegetables or plain food first, leaving the meat or strong flavor items for later. That way, the oil stays clean. When you start deep frying the savory food, the oil will turn darker and flavorful.
2. Dredge the ingredients in the batter and then panko. Remove excess panko and deep fry until crisp and golden brown.
3. Pick up the panko breadcrumbs between batches to keep the oil clean. Burnt panko will darken your oil, which will change its taste.
4. Continue with other ingredients. Use a spoon if you have a hard time coating the batter.
5. Deep fry meat and seafood at the end.
6. Drain the deep-fried food on a wire rack or paper towel. Serve immediately with Kushikatsu Sauce and Ichimi Togarashi (Japanese chili pepper).

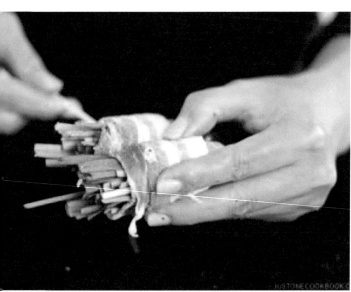

Japanese Stuffed Cabbage Rolls

Delicious and savory Japanese-Style Stuffed Cabbage Rolls served in a delicate tomato-based sauce. It's a perfect meal to share with a crowd on a cold day!

 PREP TIME: 30 Minutes   **COOK TIME:** 1 Hour

 4 SERVINGS (12 Cabbage Rolls)

Ingredients

½ **onion**

2 Tbsp **extra-virgin olive oil** (divided)

1 head **cabbage** (will need 12 cabbage leaves for 1 lb meat)

1 tsp **kosher/sea salt** (I use Diamond Crystal; Use half for table salt) (for boiling cabbage)

1 lb **ground meat** (454 g; preferably ¼ lb pork and ¾ lb beef)

1 Tbsp **all-purpose flour** (plain flour)(7.5 g)

½ Tbsp **unsalted butter** (7 g)

parsley (for garnish)

Instructions

1. Mince the onion.
2. In a frying pan, heat 1 Tbsp olive oil on medium heat and sauté onion until tender, about 4 to 6 minutes.
3. Start boiling 2 QT (2L) water and add 1 tsp salt when boiling. Remove the center core of the cabbage with a knife.
4. Completely submerge the whole cabbage and cook the cabbage until the leaves are pliable and start to peel off, about 5 minutes. Using kitchen tongs or a fork, remove the outer cabbage leaves from the pot.
5. Soak the outer cabbage leaves in iced water to stop the cooking process. Remove excess water from them with a salad spinner or pat dry with paper towel. Trim the tough, thick center vein at the base of each leaf (upside-down V shape). Alternatively, you can shave down this thick part. We will only use the large, outer leaves for wrapping. Save the smaller, inner leaves for later (Step 17).
6. Chop the thick veins into small pieces, which will be added to the stuffing.
7. In a large bowl, mix the meat, sautéed onion, and the chopped vein parts of the cabbage with your clean hands or a rubber spatula.
8. Add 1 egg, ⅓ cup panko, 2 Tbsp milk, ½ tsp nutmeg, 1 tsp salt, and pepper.
9. Mix well until the mixture is sticky and combined. Cover with plastic wrap and keep in the refrigerator for 15-30 minutes. *Tip: Optional, but this helps to keeps the meat juicy and enhances the flavor.* Try to divide the mixture into 12 equal parts.
10. Put 1 Tbsp of the flour into a fine sieve for dusting. Working with

SEASONING FOR STUFFING
1 **large egg** (50 g w/o shell)

⅓ cup **panko (Japanese breadcrumbs)** (20 g)

2 Tbsp **milk**

½ tsp **nutmeg**

1 tsp **kosher/sea salt** (I use Diamond Crystal; Use half for table salt)

⅛ tsp **freshly ground black pepper**

FOR SAUCE
2 **bay leaves**

1 clove **garlic** (minced)

1 can **diced tomatoes** (14.5-oz, 411 g)

1 Tbsp **white wine**

½ tsp **kosher/sea salt** (I use Diamond Crystal; Use half for table salt)

⅛ tsp **freshly ground black pepper**

1 cup **chicken/ vegetable stock** (240 ml)

1 leaf at a time, overlap the bottom of the cabbage leaf where you see the upside-down V-shape. Lightly dust the flour over the cabbage leaf. The flour helps the stuffing stick to the cabbage and acts as a binding agent. Add the stuffing in the center of the bottom part of the cabbage leaf.

11. Starting with the stem end, roll the cabbage up tightly, tucking in the sides of the leaf as you roll. Use one hand to pull the edge of the leaf and roll the fillings tightly toward the edge.

12. Insert a toothpick to seal and secure the edge so the roll doesn't fall apart while cooking (optional). Repeat with the remaining leaves and stuffing. *Tip: What if the cabbage leaf is broken? You can still use it. Use a smaller cabbage leaf to "patch" up and roll the fillings the same way.*

13. In a large pot (I use 6 ¾ QT oval Dutch oven), heat 1 Tbsp olive oil on medium and cook 2 bay leaves and minced garlic until fragrant. Then stir in the diced tomatoes.

14. Reduce the heat to medium-low. Add 1 Tbsp white wine, salt, and freshly ground black pepper, and bring it to a simmer on medium heat.

15. Place the cabbage rolls side by side in rows, seam side down, in the pot. If there are open spaces, stuff the leftover cabbage in the opening so the cabbage rolls won't move around while cooking. Pour 1 cup of chicken/vegetable broth.

16. Place Otoshibuta (drop lid) on top of the cabbage rolls. If you don't have a drop lid or your pot is not round, you can make one with aluminum foil. Cover to cook on medium heat. After boiling, lower the heat to medium-low and simmer for 30 minutes. Add ½ Tbsp butter to give it a little shine and more flavor.

17. When you are ready to serve, carefully pick up the stuffed cabbage roll with kitchen tongs and put in a serving dish. Remove the toothpick and pour the sauce on top. Garnish with parsley and serve.

Salmon in Foil

Salmon in Foil is a perfect dish for a busy weeknight meal! Light yet flavorful and delicious, this recipe is quick and simple to make, taking no more than 20 minutes from start to finish.

PREP TIME: 8 Minutes   **COOK TIME:** 12 Minutes   2 Servings

Ingredients

2 **fillets salmon** (roughly 8.5 oz / 240 g)

kosher/sea salt (I use Diamond Crystal; Use half for table salt)

freshly ground black pepper

½ **onion**

2 inch **carrot** (5 cm)

½ **shimeji mushrooms** (1.8 oz / 50 g)

2 **shiitake mushrooms**

2 strands **chives**

1 ½ Tbsp **unsalted butter** (divided)

1 Tbsp **sake** (divided)

2 Tbsp **ponzu or soy sauce** (for drizzling)

Instructions

TO PREPARE SALMON

1. Sprinkle kosher salt and freshly ground black pepper on both sides of the salmon fillet.
2. Thinly slice the onion and cut the carrot into julienne strips.
3. Cut off the bottom of the shimeji mushrooms and shiitake mushrooms. Break up shimeji mushrooms with your hands and thinly slice shiitake mushrooms.
4. Cut the chives into small pieces.
5. Prepare two 12" x 12" (30 x 30 cm) sheets of aluminum foil. Thinly spread the butter in the center on both sheets.
6. Place half of the onion slices and put the salmon on top, skin side down.
7. Put two kinds of mushrooms and then carrot julienne strips on top of the salmon.
8. Add ½ Tbsp sake and ½ Tbsp butter on top.
9. Bring the top and bottom aluminum foil over the salmon and fold a few times. Then bring the sides together and fold a few times to make sure the foil is sealed completely. Repeat the same process for the second salmon.

TO COOK ON THE STOVETOP

1. Place the two sets of salmon in foil on a frying pan and cover with a lid (no need to add water). Cook the salmon over medium heat for 2 minutes, then medium-low heat for 10 minutes. If you have 1 to 1 ½ inch-thick salmon, you will need to cook for 15-18 minutes (Open the foil to check the doneness).

TO BAKE IN THE OVEN

Alternatively, you can bake at preheated 425°F (218°C) oven for 15 minutes. If you have 1 to 1 ½ inch-thick salmon, you will need to cook for 18-20 minutes (Open the foil to check the doneness).

TO SERVE
Carefully open the aluminum foil to enjoy the salmon, sprinkle chives and drizzle ponzu or soy sauce on top. Enjoy!

Niratama Donburi (Chive and Egg Rice Bowl)

Start your week with this delicious Japanese comfort rice dish, Niratama donburi. Soft fluffy egg stir fry with Chinese chive served over white rice. Easy & fuss-free!

 PREP TIME: 5 Minutes   **COOK TIME:** 5 Minutes   2 Servings

Ingredients

3 **large eggs** (50 g each w/o shell)

1 tsp **sake**

½ tsp **soy sauce**

¼ tsp **kosher/sea salt** (I use Diamond Crystal; Use half for table salt)

freshly ground black pepper

2 Tbsp **neutral-flavored oil** (vegetable, canola, etc)

1.5 oz **garlic chives (Chinese chives or Nira)** (43 g) (rinsed and pat dry)

2 cups **cooked Japanese short-grain rice**

Instructions

1. Combine eggs, sake, soy sauce, salt, and black pepper in the medium bowl and mix (but do not overmix).
2. Cut the garlic chives into 2-inch (5 cm) pieces.
3. Heat ½ Tbsp oil in a wok over high heat and cook the bottom white part of garlic chives until wilted. Then add the green part and quickly stir fry.
4. Transfer the garlic chives into the bowl with the egg mixture.
5. Heat the remaining oil into the wok over high heat. When the wok is hot (smoke is coming off the wok), add the egg and garlic chive mixture into the wok. The egg mixture will get fluffy around the edges. Mix the center of the egg mixture and gently fold.
6. When the egg is almost cooked, put rice in a serving plate/bowl and transfer the egg with garlic chives over the rice.

Braised Pork Belly (Kakuni)

Kakuni (□煮) is Japanese braised pork belly, and it literary means "square simmered" referring to the shape of this dish. I'm not usually into fatty meat but there is something about this dish that I cannot resist. Slow cooking method turns the meat into a delicious creation.

 PREP TIME: 15 Minutes　　 **COOK TIME:** 3 Hours　　 4 Servings

Ingredients

1 lb **pork belly** (454 g)

1 knob **ginger** (2 inches, 5 cm)

1 **negi or 2 scallion** (long green onion)

3 **large eggs** (50 g each w/o shell)

FOR SEASONING
2 ½ cup **dashi** (Japanese soup stock) (600 ml)

4 Tbsp **sake** (60 ml)

3 Tbsp **mirin**

4 Tbsp **sugar**

4 Tbsp **soy sauce** (60 ml)

1 **dried red chili**

Instructions

1. Pound the pork on both sides with a meat pounder (or the back of the knife).
2. Then mold the meat back into the original shape with your hands, and then cut into 2-inch pieces.
3. Heat oil on the heavy skillet over medium-high and put the fattiest part on the bottom. Cook the meat until all sides are nicely browned. *Tip: Use a splatter screen to prevent the oil from splattering.*
4. When the meat is nicely browned, transfer to some paper towels and wipe off excess fat.
5. Slice the ginger and cut the green part of Tokyo negi into 2-inch pieces. Save two slices for later.
6. With the white part of Tokyo negi, make shiraga negi (page 280) for garnish.
7. In a large pot, put the seared pork belly, green part of the negi/scallion, half of the sliced ginger (save the half for later), and pour water to cover the meat.
8. Bring it to a boil and then reduce heat to simmer. Cook uncovered (so the unwanted smell goes away) for 2-3 hours, turning occasionally (if you want really tender meat, cook for at least 3 hours). When the liquid is running low, keep adding water (or hot water) to cover the meat.
9. Meanwhile make 3 hard-boiled eggs.
10. After cooking for 2 hours, drain and take out the meat and wipe off excess oil with paper towel.
11. In another large pot (I use a cast iron pot), add the pork belly, dashi, sake, and mirin. Start cooking on medium-high heat.
12. Add sugar, soy sauce, the rest of ginger slices, and the red chili pepper (I remove the seeds for my kids.).
13. When boiling, lower the heat but keep simmering. Place otoshibuta (drop

pepper

FOR OPTIONAL
TOPPINGS
**shichimi
togarashi**
(Japanese seven
spice) (for taste)

lid) on top. We'll be cooking for 1 hour on simmer/low heat.

14. After cooking for 30 minutes, add the hard-boiled eggs. Remove otoshibuta and continue simmering.

15. Simmer for another 30 minutes. Occasionally pour the sauce on top of the meat and rotate the meat and eggs. Make sure you have enough liquid so they won't get burnt. When the sauce gets reduced and the meat has a nice glaze, it's ready to serve. Serve the pork belly and eggs with shiraga negi on top.

16. If you prefer this dish to be less oily and have more flavor, wait for another day. Let cool completely and store it in the refrigerator overnight. Next day take out the pot from the refrigerator and remove the solidified fat before heating up. Heat thoroughly and serve.

Nikujaga (Meat & Potato Stew)

Nikujaga is one of the most popular Japanese comfort food. The delicious dish includes sliced beef slow cooked with potatoes, shirataki noodles, and onion.

 PREP TIME: 15 Minutes   **COOK TIME:** 15 Minutes   4 Servings

Ingredients

1 **onion**

½ **carrot**

2 **Yukon gold potatoes**

½ lb **thinly sliced beef** (chuck or rib eye) (usually beef or pork) (227 g)

1 pkg **shirataki noodles**

2-3 pecies **snow peas** (or green beans, green peas for decoration)

1 Tbsp **neutral-flavored oil** (vegetable, canola, etc)

2 cup **dashi** (Japanese soup stock) (2 cups = 480 ml)

SEASONINGS
4 Tbsp **mirin**

4 Tbsp **soy sauce**

2 Tbsp **sake**

1 Tbsp **sugar**

Instructions

1. Make dashi stock.
2. Cut the onion into 10-12 wedges. Peel and cut the carrot lengthwise in half and chop into rolling wedges.
3. Cut the potatoes into quarters and smooth the edge of potatoes. If the pieces have sharp edges then they are likely to break into pieces during the cooking process from bumping into each other. We call this Japanese cutting technique mentori. Soak the potatoes in water to remove starch.
4. Cut the sliced meat in half. Rinse and drain shirataki noodles.
5. Remove string from snow peas and cook them in boiling water for 30 seconds and take them out.
6. Then cook shirataki noodles in the boiling water for 1 minute and cut in half.
7. In a large pot, heat oil on medium heat and sauté the onion.
8. When the onion is coated with oil, add the meat and cook until no longer pink.
9. Add the potatoes, carrots, and shirataki noodles.
10. Add dashi stock and seasonings. Bring to a boil.
11. Once boiling, skim the scum and foam. Make sure all the ingredients are flat and most of the ingredients are just covered by the broth.
12. Place an otoshibuta (drop lid) or make one with aluminum foil, and simmer on medium-low heat for 10-15 minutes, or until vegetables are cooked. Otoshibuta is necessary to maintain the shape of the vegetables. Do not mix the ingredients while cooking; Otoshibuta will help the flavor circulate automatically.
13. Turn off the heat and discard the otoshibuta. Let it stand for 30 minutes before serving. The flavors will soak into the

ingredients while cooling down. If you don't have time for this, it's also okay.

14. When reheating, pour the soup on top of the ingredients with a spoon a couple of times. Check the flavors for the last time. When it's almost ready, toss in the snow peas to warm them up. When ingredients are heated through, it's ready to serve.

Chikuzenni (Nishime) – Simmered Chicken and Vegetables

Chikuzenni is a dish with chicken and vegetables simmered in flavorful dashi, mirin, and soy sauce. It's one of the Osechi Ryori (Japanese traditional food) served on New Year's Day.

 PREP TIME: 1 Hour   **COOK TIME:** 30 Minutes   6 Servings

Ingredients

6 **dried shiitake mushrooms** (1 oz, 30 g)

1 cup **water** (240 ml; for rehydrating dried shiitake mushrooms)

¾ lb **boneless, skinless chicken thighs** (340 g)

½ Tbsp **sake** (for marinating chicken)

½ Tbsp **soy sauce** (for marinating chicken)

1 **lotus root (renkon)** (6 oz, 180 g)

½ **gobo (burdock root)** (4 oz, 110 g)

1 Tbsp **rice vinegar** (separated; for soaking lotus root and gobo)

5 **taro (satoimo)** (9 oz, 250

Instructions

DRIED SHIITAKE MUSHROOMS

1. In a small bowl, put dried shiitake mushrooms and 1 cup water and soak for 20-30 minutes, or until tender.
2. After 30 minutes or so, squeeze the liquid out from the shiitake mushrooms.
3. Cut the shiitake mushrooms into hexagons (The shape resembles a turtle for longevity).
4. Strain the liquid through a fine-mesh sieve. This is called shiitake dashi. It yields roughly ¾ cup.

CHICKEN

1. Remove extra fat from the chicken and cut into 1 ½ inch (3.8 cm) pieces.
2. Transfer the chicken to a medium bowl and add ½ Tbsp sake and ½ Tbsp soy sauce. Coat the chicken with the marinade and set aside.

BURDOCK ROOT (GOBO)

1. Scrape the skin off the burdock root with the back of the knife. After rinsing, cut it into thin slices.
2. Prepare bowl with 2 cups water and ½ Tbsp vinegar. Soak the burdock root in the water for 15 minutes.

JAPANESE TARO ROOTS (SATOIMO)

1. Cut off the ends of the taro. Then peel from one end to the other.
2. Ideally, taro should be a hexagon (6 sides) from the side

g)

½ **boiled bamboo shoot** (3 oz, 90 g)

1 **carrot** (6 oz, 170 g)

½ block **konnyaku (konjac)** (4.5 oz, 130 g)

10 **snow peas** (1 oz, 30 g)

⅛ tsp **kosher/sea salt** (I use Diamond Crystal; Use half for table salt) (for blanching snow peas)

1 ½ Tbsp **sesame oil** (roasted) (separated)

SEASONINGS
2 cups **dashi** (Japanese soup stock) (480 ml)

3 Tbsp **sake** (45 ml)

3 Tbsp **mirin** (45 ml)

1 Tbsp **sugar**

3 Tbsp **usukuchi (lightcolor) soy sauce** (or use 2 Tbsp soy sauce + ⅛ tsp salt)(45 ml)

½ tsp **kosher/sea salt** (I use Diamond Crystal; Use half for table salt)

view.
3. Cut the taro in half and soak in water. (Optionally, you can rub them with salt to get rid of the sliminess).

BAMBOO SHOOT
Cut the bamboo shoot into quarters lengthwise and in half widthwise. If each piece is still bigger than bite-size, you can cut in half.

LOTUS ROOTS (RENKON)
1. Cut the lotus root into Hana Renkon.
2. The lotus root should resemble flowers after cutting the edges off.
3. Cut them into ⅛ inch (3 mm) slices and soak them in water (2 cups water + ½ Tbsp vinegar).

CARROT (NEJIRI UME)
1. Peel the carrot and cut into ½ inch pieces.
2. Use a flower-shaped vegetable cutter and cut out each piece into a flower shape. Then make a shallow (roughly ¼ inch deep) incision from the center of the flower to in-between the two petals.
3. Hold a knife parallel to one petal and make a diagonal cut from right to left in-between petals.
4. This is called Nejiri Ume.

KONNYAKU
1. Cut konnyaku into ¼ inch slices and then make a 1 ½ inch incision in the middle.
2. Put one end of konnyaku into the hole in the middle and pull it out. This is called Tazuna Konnyaku.

SNOW PEAS
1. Pull the strings at the seams of the snow peas, and discard. These are tough and not edible.

TO BLANCH VEGETABLES AND KONNYAKU
1. Boil water in a saucepan and blanch half of the flower carrot for 2 minutes and set aside.
2. Add a pinch of salt and blanch the snow pea pods for 30-60 seconds, until crisp but tender enough to eat.
3. Remove the snow peas from the water and transfer to the ice water to stop cooking and set aside.
4. In the same boiling water, add konnyaku. After boiling again,

cook for 2-3 minutes to remove the smell.

5. Diagonally cut the blanched snow peas in half and set aside.

TO MAKE CHIKUZENNI

1. In the large pot, heat 1 Tbsp of sesame oil over medium heat. When it's hot, add the chicken.
2. Cook the chicken until it turns white. Transfer the chicken to a plate.
3. Add ½ Tbsp sesame oil and cook all the ingredients except the blanched snow peas and carrots reserved for decoration.
4. Stir and coat the ingredients with sesame oil.
5. Add dashi and shiitake dashi.
6. Bring it to a simmer over medium heat. Skim off the fat and scum that accumulate on the surface .
7. Add sake, mirin, sugar, soy sauce, and salt.
8. Add the chicken back into the pot. Bring it to a simmer. The stock should cover about 80% of the ingredients.
9. Put an otoshibuta (drop lid) on the ingredients and cook for 10 minutes. If you don't have one, you can make an otoshibuta with aluminum foil .
10. Remove otoshibuta and cook for another 10 minutes.
11. Insert a bamboo skewer into tough vegetables (taro root and lotus root) and see if they are tender. Taste and adjust seasonings if needed.

TO SERVE AND STORE

Add the snow peas and remove from the heat. Cover, and let cool. Serve Chikuzenni in a serving dish or Osechi box. Top with the snow peas and blanched flower shaped carrots.

Chashu (Japanese Braised Pork Belly)

Make this easy, melt-in-mouth Chashu pork belly recipe at home! Braised in a sweet and savory sauce, you can now add the tender slice of meat as topping to your next bowl of ramen!

 PREP TIME: 20 Minutes   **COOK TIME:** 2 Hours 20 Minutes   8 Servings

Ingredients

FOR ROLLED CHASHU (LOG) (SERVES 8-10)
2-2½ lb **pork belly block** (907-1134 g/roughly 8" x 9")

1 **negi (long green onion)** (Sub: 1 leek or 2-3 green onions)

1 knob **ginger**

1 Tbsp **neutral-flavored oil** (vegetable, canola, etc)

1 cup **sake** (240 ml)

1 cup **soy sauce** (240 ml)

2 cup **water** (480 ml)

⅔ cup **sugar** (150 g)

FOR NON-ROLLED CHASHU (BLOCK) (SERVES 3; THIS IS THE ORIGINAL RECIPE POSTED ON MAY 2011)
¾ lb **pork belly block** (340 g)

Instructions

FOR ROLLED CHASHU
(NON-ROLLED VERSION AT THE END)

DAY 1

TO PREPARE THE PORK BELLY

1. Roll up the pork belly, making sure one or both ends should have a "bacon-like" appearance, showing the varying layers of meat and fat. If your slab comes with the skin (rind), it should be removed. Ask your butcher and they may remove it for you.
2. Run some butcher twine under the far end of the log. Tie a double knot to secure the pork tightly. Make sure you leave about 3 inches (7.5 cm) twine at the end.
3. Wrap around the pork belly 2-3 times around the same area to secure the end. Then pull the twine to the other end of the pork belly. Wrap around 2-3 times at the end area to secure before working toward the middle. Each wrap should be a ⅓ inch (1 cm) in between.
4. Continue wrapping around the pork belly toward the end (where you started). Make sure it's wrapped as tightly as possible.
5. Once you reach the end, run the butcher twine under some wraps to hook and go back to the starting point. Find the 3-inch (7.5 cm) twine you leave behind.
6. Tie a double knot with the long twine and the 3-inch (7.5 cm) twine.

TO CUT AROMATICS

1. Cut off the green part of the long green onion and slice the

1 **negi (long green onion)**
(Sub: 1 leek or 2-3 green
onions)

1 knob **ginger**

½ Tbsp **neutral-flavored oil**
(vegetable, canola, etc)

⅓ cup **sake** (80 ml)

⅓ cup **soy sauce** (80 ml)

⅔ cup **water** (160 ml)

3 Tbsp **sugar** (45 g)

ginger.

TO SEAR THE PORK BELLY

1. Heat the oil in a cast iron skillet (or regular frying pan) over high heat. Add the rolled pork belly in the pan.
2. Sear the pork belly one side at a time, rotating to make sure all sides are nicely seared.
3. It'll take about 10-15 minutes all together.

TO PREPARE THE SAUCE

While searing, put all the ingredients for seasonings in a heavy-bottom pot that fits the chashu.

TO SIMMER CHASHU

1. Transfer the seared chashu into the Dutch oven.
2. Bring the liquid to a boil.
3. Once boiling, skim off the foam and scum. Then turn the heat to a low simmer.
4. Put an otoshibuta (drop lid) on top to press ingredients down. It helps to limit the evaporation. If you don't have an otoshibuta, you can make it with aluminum foil.
5. Simmer on low heat and cover with otoshibuta at all times for the next 2 hours, rotating chashu every 30 minutes.
6. Once t he sauce has been reduced, after 2 hours, turn off the heat to let cool a little bit.

TO REST CHASHU OVERNIGHT

1. Once the meat is slightly cooled, transfer to a container or plastic Food Saver bag. Strain the leftover cooking liquid over a fine-mesh strainer. The liquid is roughly 2 ½ cup.
2. Add ½ cup of the cooking liquid into the bag.
3. Seal the bag with Food Saver. *TIP: Fold a piece of paper towel to plug the entry of the Food Saver bag. This paper towel will absorb all the moisture and prevent leaking.*
4. I usually make ramen eggs (Ajitsuke Tamago) with the leftover liquid. Simply make soft boiled eggs and add ½ cup of cooking liquid in the bag. Cover the cooking liquid and store the chashu, ramen egg, and the cooking liquid in the refrigerator.

DAY 2

1. Open the bag of chashu.
2. Cut the twine with kitchen shears and remove them completely.

3. Slice the chashu into ¼ inch pieces (Keep the edge for chashu fried rice!).

4. Place the chashu slices on a ceramic plate and use a propane torch or broiler to sear the chashu slices to enhance the flavor. Enjoy them immediately or serve on your ramen.

5. Scoop up the solidified fat from the cooking sauce.

6. Prepare a mason jar or container and strain the sauce over a fine-mesh sieve to make sure the solidified fat is left behind. The sauce will last for a month in the refrigerator. I use it for drizzling over the chashu and making stir-fries, marinade, and ramen eggs.

TO STORE

You can store the chashu in the refrigerator up to 7 days and 1 month in the freezer. I usually divide the rolled chashu into thirds and freeze 2 portions separately (for ramen right away, and chashu fried rice and chashu don for later). Ramen eggs should be consumed in 3-4 days if they are soft-boiled eggs and 7 days if hard-boiled. The eggs get salty as you keep them in the marinade, so remove from the sauce when they have the right taste.

FOR NON-ROLLED CHASHU

1. Gather all the ingredients. For small blocks of pork belly, you don't need to roll them up before cooking, and the simmering time is just 1 hour (instead of 2 hours).

2. Heat the oil in a cast iron skillet (or regular frying pan) over high heat. Sear the fat side down first, then flip over to sear all sides, which will take about 10 minutes.

3. While searing, put all the seasoning ingredients in a heavy-bottom pot (or regular pot) that fits the chashu. Add the chashu and bring it to a boil, skimming the scum and foam. Then turn the heat to low.

4. Put an otoshibuta (drop lid) on top to press the ingredients down and to limit the evaporation. If you don't have an otoshibuta, you can make it with aluminum foil. Simmer on low heat for one hour, rotating chashu every 15 minutes (keep otoshibuta on all times!).

5. After one hour, there should be ½ inch liquid left in the pot. Now you have 2 options. **Option 1:** If you're serving right away, remove the otoshibuta and further cook down the sauce on low heat until thickened and you can see the bottom of the pot when you draw a line with a spatula. **Option 2 (recommended):** Transfer the chashu to a container or a bag

with a little bit of cooking sauce and refrigerate overnight. Strain the leftover cooking sauce and refrigerate.

6. To serve, slice the chashu into ¼ inch pieces. You can use a propane torch or broiler to sear the chashu slices to enhance the flavor. If you kept the chashu overnight and don't want to sear it, you can reheat it by soaking in the hot cooking sauce.

RICE (+NOODLES)

Baked Katsudon (Japanese Crispy Baked Cutlet Rice Bowl)

Crispy pork cutlet simmered in runny egg with a dashi broth, and served over hot steamed rice, this Baked Katsudon recipe is the rice bowl of your dream. Learn how to make the best crunchy cutlet without deep frying.

 PREP TIME: 25 Minutes   **COOK TIME:** 40 Minutes   2 Servings

Ingredients

FOR BAKED KATSU:
1 cup **panko (Japanese breadcrumbs)** (60 g)

1 Tbsp **neutral-flavored oil** (vegetable, canola, etc)

2 pieces **boneless pork loin chops** (½ inch thick) (½ lb or 226 g; thickness is 1.2 cm or ½")

1 tsp **kosher/sea salt** (I use Diamond Crystal; Use half for table salt)

freshly ground black pepper

2 Tbsp **all-purpose flour** (plain flour)(15 g)

1 **large egg** (50 g w/o shell)

Instructions

Adjust the oven rack to the middle position and preheat the oven to 400°F (200°C).

TO MAKE TONKATSU

1. Combine the panko and oil in a frying pan and toast over medium heat until golden brown. Transfer panko into a shallow dish and allow to cool.
2. Cut the onions into thin slices and the mitsuba into small pieces.
3. Remove the extra fat and make a couple of slits on the connective tissue between the meat and fat. The red meat and fat have different elasticity, and when they are cooked they will shrink and expand at different rates. This will allow tonkatsu to stay nice and flat and prevent it from curling up.
4. Pound the meat with a meat pounder, or the back of a knife. Mold the extended meat back into the original shape with your hands.
5. Sprinkle salt and freshly ground black pepper.
6. Dredge each pork piece in the flour to coat completely. Pat off the excess flour.
7. Beat one egg in a bowl and coat the pork with the beaten egg. Finally, coat with the toasted panko. Press on the panko flakes to make sure they adhere to the pork.
8. Place the pork on the prepared baking sheet lined with parchment paper or, even better, an oven-safe wire rack (this allows air to flow through the bottom so panko won't get crushed). Bake at 400°F (200°C) until the pork is no longer pink inside, about 20 minutes.

FOR KATSUDON:
½ **onion** (divided - ¼ onion/serving)

2 **large eggs** (50 g each w/o shell) (divided - 1 egg/serving)

2 servings cooked **Japanese short-grain rice**

FOR KATSUDON SAUCE (DIVIDED FOR EACH SERVING):
1 cup **dashi** (Japanese soup stock) (240 ml)

2 Tbsp **sake**

2 Tbsp **mirin**

2 Tbsp **soy sauce**

2 tsp **sugar**

TO SERVE:
mitsuba (Japanese parsley)

shichimi togarashi (Japanese seven spice) (optional)

9. Remove the tonkatsu from the oven and cut into 1-inch pieces (so you can eat with chopsticks).

TO PREPARE SAUCE AND EGG

Combine Seasonings in a liquid measuring cup or bowl. This amount could be more than you need, depending on the size of your frying pan. You can store the extra in a mason jar in the refrigerator for up to a week. Beat one egg in a bowl.

WHY DO WE USE OYAKODON PAN?

Traditionally, katsudon is made in a 1-serving Oyakodon Pan. Why? The size of the oyakodon pan is similar to a donburi bowl size; therefore, it's easy to slide the cooked food over steamed rice in the bowl. You can make 2 servings at once in one large frying pan and carefully divide it, but each portion won't be a round shape to fit over the round rice bowl.

TO MAKE KATSUDON

1. Put half of the onion slices into the pan and pour ½ to ¾ cup of the sauce to cover them. Adjust the amount of sauce based on your frying pan size. Bring the sauce and onions to a boil. Lower the heat to medium and cook onion slices until translucent, about 4-5 minutes.
2. Put one baked tonkatsu in it and turn the heat to medium-high. Pour and distribute beaten egg evenly and cover with the lid.
3. When the egg is half cooked, about 30 seconds, turn off the heat.

TO SERVE

Serve rice in a donburi bowl and slide tonkatsu and egg mixture on top. Continue with the second serving. Serve with shichimi togarashi (Japanese seven spice) on the side.

Unadon (Unagi Donburi)

Have fun making one of the Japanese favorites, Unadon (grilled eel rice bowl), in your own kitchen. Sweet caramelized homemade unagi sauce drizzled over perfectly grilled unagi and steamed rice, this recipe will make any Japanese food enthusiasts mouth water.

 PREP TIME: 10 Minutes   **COOK TIME:** 10 Minutes   4 Servings

Ingredients

2 fillets **unagi (eel)** (1 fillet = 160 g or 5.6 oz) (defrosted)

Japanese sansho pepper (for toppings; optional)

UNAGI SAUCE (UNAGI TARE):
¼ cup **soy sauce** (Use GF soy sauce for Gluten Free)(60 ml)

¼ cup **mirin** (60 ml)

2 ½ Tbsp **sugar**

1 ½ Tbsp **sake**

Instructions

TO MAKE UNAGI SAUCE

1. In a small saucepan, add mirin, sake, and sugar. Turn on the heat to medium and whisk the mixture to combine.
2. Then add soy sauce and bring it to a boil. Once boiling, reduce heat to the low and continue simmering for 10 minutes, or until the sauce slightly thickens. Toward the end of cooking, you will see more bubbles.
3. Remove from the heat. As it cools, the sauce will thicken more. You can store the sauce in an airtight jar and keep in the refrigerator for up to 2 weeks.

TO BROIL

1. Preheat the broiler* to medium (500°F/260°C) with a rack placed about 6-inch (15 cm) away from the top heating element (in the center of the oven) for 5 minutes. I usually use medium (6-inch away) or high (8-inch away). When broiling, you don't control the temperature in the oven; instead, you control the distance between the heating element and the surface of the food. It's similar to using hotter and cooler zones on your grill. *Broiler setting: Low (450°F/232°C), Medium (500°F/260°C), and High (550°F/288°C).*
2. Line a baking sheet with foil for easy cleaning (Brush/spray the foil with oil). Cut the unagi in half (or thirds, depending on the serving bowl size) and place it on the foil, skin side down. Broil it at medium setting (500°F/260°C) until the surface is slightly blistered, about 5-7 minutes. No need to flip.
3. After 5-7 minutes, open the oven and brush the unagi with the sauce.
4. Broil again for 30-60 seconds until you see bubbles on top of unagi.

TO BAKE

Preheat the oven to 425°F/218°C with a rack placed in the middle, and bake the unagi on parchment paper until the surface is slightly blistered, about 10-12 minutes. No need to flip.

TO PAN FRY

Wrap the unagi in foil (similar to this recipe) and reheat on low heat for 5-8 minutes. You won't get nice blisters/chars if you use this method.

TO SERVE

Serve rice in a bowl and pour or brush unagi sauce on therice. Place unagi on top of rice and pour/brush more unagi sauce. Serve immediately. Optionally, you can sprinkle Japanese sansho pepper on top.

Soboro Don (Ground Chicken Bowl)

Soboro Don is usually served at the end of a meal at yakitori restaurants in Japan. It's typically just the ground chicken over rice; however, at home, this dish consists of ground chicken, eggs, and some green veggies to make it more colorful.

 PREP TIME: 10 Minutes   **COOK TIME:** 20 Minutes   2 Servings (3 if small bowls)

Ingredients

FOR GROUND CHICKEN
1 Tbsp **neutral-flavored oil** (vegetable, canola, etc)

½ lb **ground chicken** (227 g; you can also mince the chicken thighs (or use a food processor). I recommend using thighs.)

1 tsp **ginger** (grated, with juice)

1 Tbsp **sake**

1 ½ Tbsp **sugar** (Use 1 Tbsp if you prefer less sweet)

1 Tbsp **mirin**

2 Tbsp **soy sauce**

FOR SCRAMBLED EGGS
2 **large eggs** (50 g each w/o shell)

1 Tbsp **sugar**

1 Tbsp **neutral-flavored oil** (vegetable, canola, etc)

TO SERVE

Instructions

1. Heat oil in a non-stick frying pan on medium heat, and cook the chicken until no longer pink. Using a wooden spoon, break up the meat into small pieces.
2. Add sake, sugar, and mirin.
3. Add soy sauce and continue to break up the meat into smaller pieces.
4. Grate ginger and keep the juice. When the meat is broken up to pieces, add the ginger with juice.
5. Cook until the liquid is almost gone. Transfer to a bowl and set aside and wash the frying pan.
6. Beat the eggs in a small bowl and add sugar. Mix well until the sugar is completely dissolved. Prepare several long cooking chopsticks.
7. Heat oil in the frying pan over medium-low heat and pour in the egg mixture.
8. Hold several chopsticks in one hand and break the egg into small pieces. When it's cooked, transfer to another bowl. Now you have three ingredients in separate bowls.
9. Serve steamed rice in serving bowls and put the three toppings on top of the rice as you like. Garnish with pickled ginger (kizami shoga). Enjoy!

2 servings **cooked Japanese short-grain rice**

¼ cup **green peas** (defrosted)(36 g)

pickled red ginger (beni shoga or kizami beni shoga)

Soy-Glazed Eggplant Donburi

With thinly sliced eggplant seared till golden brown and coated with sweet soy sauce, this Soy-Glazed Eggplant Donburi is an incredibly delicious Japanese vegan rice bowl. Just 20 minutes start to finish!

 PREP TIME: 10 Minutes   **COOK TIME:** 10 Minutes   2 Servings

Ingredients

7 oz **Japanese/Chinese eggplant** (200 g; 2 Japanese eggplants)

10 **Shiso leaves** (Ooba) (or use 1 green onion)

1 knob **ginger**

2 Tbsp **potato starch/cornstarch**

4 Tbsp **neutral-flavored oil** (vegetable, canola, etc) (separated; use 2 Tbsp at a time) (60 ml)

½ tsp **toasted white sesame seeds**

SEASONINGS
4 Tbsp **mirin** (Not exactly same, but can substitute with 4 tsp sugar + 4 Tbsp sake/water; Please adjust the sweetness based on your preference)

2 Tbsp **soy sauce** (or use GF

Instructions

1. Slice eggplant into ¼ inch slices and sprinkle with salt (roughly ½-1 tsp). Set aside for 15 minutes and wipe off the moisture with a paper towel.
2. Rinse the shiso leaves and dry with a paper towel. Discard the stems.
3. Roll up the shiso leaves and cut into chiffonade.
4. Peel and grate the ginger. You'll need 1 tsp ginger.
5. Put 2 Tbsp potato starch in a small tray and thinly coat the eggplant slices on both sides.
6. Heat the 2 Tbsp oil in a frying pan over medium heat. When the oil is hot, add the eggplant slices in a single layer. Cook until the bottom side is golden brown, about 3-4 minutes. Until then, do not touch the eggplants to achieve a nice sear.
7. When the bottom side is nicely seared, drizzle the rest of oil (2 Tbsp) on top and flip the eggplant slices to cook the other side, about 3-4 minutes.
8. Once this side is cooked till golden brown, reduce the heat to medium-low heat and add mirin, soy sauce, and grated ginger.
9. Bring it back to simmer and spoon the sauce over the eggplant a few times. If the sauce thickens too fast (due to the potato starch), add 1 Tbsp water at a time to loosen slightly. Remove from the heat when the eggplant is well-coated with the sauce.
10. Serve steamed rice in a donburi bowl (a bit bigger than rice bowl) and drizzle some sauce.
11. Then place the eggplant slices on top. For presentation, I overlap each slice slightly. Garnish with shiso leaves and

soy sauce for gluten free)

sprinkle sesame seeds on top. Serve immediately.

Japanese Chicken Curry

Delicious Japanese chicken curry recipe for a weeknight dinner! Tender pieces of chicken, carrots and potatoes cooked in a rich savory curry sauce, this Japanese version of curry is a mustkeep for your family meal.

 PREP TIME: 30 Minutes   **COOK TIME:** 1 Hour   8 Servings

Ingredients

1.5 lb **boneless, skinless chicken thighs** (680 g or beef, pork, seafood, tofu, or more vegetables; you can increase up to 2 lbs/907 g)

kosher/sea salt (I use Diamond Crystal; Use half for table salt)

freshly ground black pepper

2 **carrots**

2 **onions**

1-2 **potatoes** (2-3 yukon gold potatoes if you want to preserve the potato shape)

½ Tbsp **ginger** (grated)

2 cloves **garlic**

1 ½ Tbsp **neutral flavored oil** (vegetable, canola, etc)

4 cups **chicken stock/broth** (960 ml)

1 **apple** (I used Fuji apple)

1 Tbsp **honey**

Instructions

1. Discard the extra fat from the chicken and cut it into bite size pieces. Season with pinches of salt and pepper.
2. Peel and cut the carrot in rolling wedges *(rangiri)* and cut the onions in wedges.
3. Cut the potatoes into 1.5 inch (4 cm) pieces and soak in water for 15 minutes to remove excess starch.
4. Grate the ginger and crush the garlic.
5. Heat the oil in a large pot over medium heat and sauté the onions until they become translucent.
6. Add the ginger and garlic. Then add the chicken and cook until the chicken is no longer pink.
7. Add the carrot and mix.
8. Add the chicken broth and bring it to a boil. Different chicken broth brands contain different amount of salt. If you need to be careful with sodium intake, you can use water only or use half stock + half water. You can always add salt at the end of cooking. Bring the stock to boil and skim the scrum and fat from the surface.
9. Peel the apple and grate it (use as much as you like to add sweetness)
10. Add the honey and salt and simmer uncovered for 20 minutes, stirring occasionally. Add the potatoes and cook for 15 minutes, or until the potatoes are tender, and turn off the heat.
11. When the potatoes are ready, add the curry. Put 1-2 blocks of roux in a ladle and slowly let it dis-

½ tsp **kosher/sea salt** (I use Diamond Crystal; Use half for table salt)

1 box **Japanese curry roux** (7 oz or 200 g)

1 ½ Tbsp **soy sauce**

1 Tbsp **ketchup**

TOPPINGS:
soft/hard-boiled egg

Fukujinzuke (red pickled daikon)

solve with a spoon or chopsticks. Continue with the rest of the roux.

12. Add the roux paste back into the stock in the large pot and stir to combine.

13. Add soy sauce and ketchup. Simmer uncovered on low heat, stirring occasionally, until the curry becomes thick.

14. Serve the curry with Japanese rice on the side and garnish with soft boiled egg and Fukujinzuke. You can store the curry in the refrigerator up to 2-3 days and in the freezer for 1 month. Potatoes will change in texture so you can take them out before freezing.

Instant Pot Cream Stew

This creamy, hearty, and delicious Japanese Cream Stew is a popular western-style (yoshoku) dish consisting of chicken and vegetables with a savory white sauce. Cooked in the Instant Pot, it's a true comfort food in cold winter months!

 PREP TIME: 20 Minutes   **COOK TIME:** 1 Hour   4 Servings

Ingredients

1 lb **chicken thigh** (454 g) (substitute with more vegetables for vegetarian)

½ tsp **kosher/sea salt** (I use Diamond Crystal; Use half for table salt)

freshly ground black pepper

2 **potatoes** (I used russet potatoes)

1 **carrot**

1 **onion**

4-5 **mushrooms**

1 head **broccoli** (420 g)

1 Tbsp **olive oil**

1 Tbsp **unsalted butter** (14 g)

1 ¾ cup **chicken broth** (400 ml)(or vegetable broth)

Instructions

PREPARE STEW INGREDIENTS
1.   Peel and cut each potato into big chunks.
2.   Peel the carrot and cut into smaller chunks. I use *rangiri* Japanese cutting technique.
3.   Cut the onion in half lengthwise, and then cut each half into 6 wedges. Finally, cut them in half widthwise.
4.   Slice the mushrooms and cut the head of broccoli into florets.
5.   Cut the chicken thighs into smaller pieces. I use *sogigiri* Japanese cutting technique to create more surface space so the chicken pieces cook faster. Season the chicken with salt and freshly ground black pepper.

TO COOK INGREDIENTS IN INSTANT POT
1.   Press the "Sauté" button on your Instant Pot and heat 1 Tbsp olive oil and 1 Tbsp unsalted butter.
2.   When the pot is hot and butter is melted, add the chicken.
3.   Stir and coat the chicken with oil.
4.   Add the onion, carrot, mushrooms, and potatoes.
5.   Add the chicken broth and 1 bay leaf.
6.   Close the lid and set HIGH pressure for 2 minutes.
7.   Make sure the steam release handle points at "sealing" and not "venting". The float valve goes up when pressurized.

TO COOK INGREDIENTS IN THE POT OVER THE STOVE
Heat the olive oil and butter in the pot over medium heat. Add the chicken and sauté for 2 minutes. Then add

1 **bay leaf**

WHITE SAUCE
3 Tbsp **unsalted butter** (42 g)

3 Tbsp **all-purpose flour**
(plain flour) (23 g)

⅛ tsp **white pepper powder**
(highly recommend!)

**freshly ground black
pepper**

½ - 1 tsp **kosher/sea salt** (I
use Diamond Crystal; Use
half for table salt)

1 cup **milk** (240 ml)(I used 2%
lactose milk)

onion and carrot and cook until coated with oil. Add the mushrooms, potatoes, broth (3.5 cups/800 ml), and bay leaf. Bring it to boil, then reduce heat to a simmer (low) and cook for 20 minutes, or until carrots and potatoes are tender.

TO BLANCH BROCCOLI
1. While pressure cooking, blanch the broccoli. Bring water to a boil in a small saucepan. Once boiling, add a pinch of salt and the broccoli florets.
2. Cook until tender but do not overcook. Transfer the broccoli to ice water to stop cooking further. Once cool, remove, drain, and set aside.

TO MAKE WHITE SAUCE (BECHAMEL SAUCE)
1. In a saucepan, melt the butter on medium heat but don't let it brown. Microwave 1 cup of milk until it is warm to the touch and set aside.
2. Once the butter is melted completely, add the flour.
3. Stir quickly and constantly with a whisk to combine. Cook the flour mixture for 3-4 minutes without letting it brown.
4. Pour a small amount of the warm milk at a time, and stir as the sauce thickens.
5. Gradually add the rest of the milk by whisking continously until smooth. Cook, stirring constantly, until starting to bubble and thicken.
6. Lower the heat and add white pepper and salt to taste.
7. Cook, stirring constantly, for 2 to 3 minutes. Remove from the heat and set aside.

ONCE PRESSURE COOKING IS DONE...
1. When it's finished cooking, the Instant Pot will switch automatically to the "Keep Warm" mode. Let the pressure release naturally for 15 minutes and then proceed with the quick release by turning the steam release handle to the "venting" position to let steam out until the float valve drops down. *Tip: Hold a kitchen towel and do not place your hand or face over the steam release valve. There should only be a little bit of steam left after 15 minutes of natural release.*
2. Open the lid and insert a skewer in the center of the potato to see if it's cooked through.
3. Using a ladle, take out 1 cup of soup from the stew.
4. Put the white sauce back on the stove and heat on low

heat. Add several tablespoons of the soup and whisk well to combine.

5. Gradually add the rest of the soup, stirring constantly, to combine.
6. Put the white sauce back in the instant pot and gently mix the white sauce with the rest of the stew.
7. Press the "Sauté" button on your Instant Pot and press "Adjust" to set "Less" heat.
8. The stew will thicken as it's heated. Season with freshly ground black pepper and discard the bay leaf.
9. Add the blanched broccoli and heat up. Serve the steamed rice on one side of the bowl and pour the Cream Stew on the other side of the bowl.

Meat Doria (Rice Gratin)

Similar to gratin, Doria is the savory meat sauce over steamed rice, covered with melted cheese and baked in the oven. This Yoshoku (Japanese western meal) is a comfort dish from childhood to many Japanese.

 PREP TIME: 15 Minutes   **COOK TIME:** 45 Minutes   4 Servings (to 6 as main dish)

Ingredients

2 rice cooker cups **Japanese short-grain rice** (360 ml)

FOR MEAT MIXTURE
½ **onion**

1 stalk **celery**

1 **carrot**

6 **mushrooms**

12 oz **beef** (preferably beef 70% & pork 30%)(340 g)

1 can **diced tomatoes** (14.5 oz)(411 g)

3-4 cups **Vegetable stock** (or chicken stock; You need the broth just enough to cover the ingredients, not ALL 4 cups in the recipe)(720 - 960 ml)

FOR SEASONINGS
2 Tbsp **extra-virgin olive oil**

1 **bay leaf**

4 Tbsp **red wine** (60 ml)

½ tsp **sugar**

Instructions

1. Start cooking rice using a rice cooker, instant pot, or a pot over the stove top.
2. Finely chop the onion, celery, carrot, and, parsley and slice the mushrooms.
3. In a large skillet, heat oil on medium-high and cook the bay leaf until fragrant. Then sauté the onion and the celery until soft.
4. Add the mushroom and the carrot and cook until soft.
5. Add the meat and pour in the red wine. Use a wooden spoon to break up the meat.
6. When the meat is almost cooked, add tomatoes with their juice and the sugar. Then add vegetable broth just enough until all the ingredients are just covered.
7. Add ketchup and tonkatsu sauce and bring it to a boil.
8. Remove excess fat from the soup.
9. Reduce heat to medium-low and simmer (without a lid) until most liquid is evaporated. When you move the meat sauce and see the bottom of the skillet, it's done cooking. Add the butter and season with salt and pepper.
10. Butter the baking dish(es) and add in steamed rice.
11. Pour the meat sauce on top of rice. Then sprinkle 2 kinds of cheese and Panko on top.
12. Set the oven setting to broil (high) and broil for 2-3 minutes until the cheese is nicely melted and turns golden. Garnish with parsley and serve.

3 Tbsp **Ketchup**

3 Tbsp **Tonkatsu sauce** (or Worcestershire sauce)

1 Tbsp **unsalted butter** (14 g)

kosher/sea salt (I use Diamond Crystal; Use half for table salt)

freshly ground black pepper

FOR TOPPINGS
¾-1 cup **Mozzarella cheese** (113 g)

¾-1 cup **Parmesan cheese** (85 g)

2-3 Tbsp **panko** (Japanese breadcrumbs)

parsley (fresh, to garnish)

Easy Fried Rice (Gluten Free)

This classic Fried Rice recipe with ham, egg, and green onion is a delicious one-pan meal that you can whip up under 20 minutes. It's bursting with flavor and perfect for a weeknight meal.

 PREP TIME: 5 Minutes　　 **COOK TIME:** 10 Minutes　　 1 Serving (as main dish)

Ingredients

2 rice bowls **cooked Japanese short-grain rice** (Ideally a day old, See blog post)

2 slices **ham**

1 **green onion/scallion**

1 **large egg** (50 g w/o shell)

2 Tbsp **neutral-flavored oil** (vegetable, canola, etc) (divided)

½ tsp **kosher/sea salt** (I use Diamond Crystal; Use half for table salt) (¼ tsp if using table salt)

white pepper powder (a must have for my fried rice!)

2 tsp **soy sauce** (I use Kikkoman® Gluten Free Tamari Soy Sauce)

Instructions

PREPARATION

1. To prepare steamed rice, microwave your one-day-old rice that's kept in the refrigerator until room temperature or warm. If you do not have one-day-old rice, then you can cook the rice, spread it out on a baking sheet lined with parchment paper, and leave it out on the counter without cover for 1-2 hours. This will remove moisture in the rice.
2. Cut the white part of the green onion into rounds and the green part diagonally, dividing the white and green parts.
3. Cut the ham into ¼ inch square pieces.
4. Crack and whisk the egg in a bowl.

COOKING

1. Make sure all the ingredients are ready to go. Heat the wok (or the large frying pan) on medium-high. Once it's hot, add 1 Tbsp oil and swirl around to make sure all sides of the wok (frying pan) are coated with oil. Add the beaten egg and mix around so it becomes fluffy.
2. While some parts of the egg are still a little bit runny (not all the way cooked), transfer to a plate. We do not want to overcook the egg at this stage.
3. Add 1 Tbsp oil and start cooking ham and white parts of the chopped green onion. Stir fry and coat well with oil.
4. Add the room temp/warm rice into the wok (frying pan). Separate the rice with a spatula, without damaging the rice. Don't make it mushy by pressing down, but fluff out the rice so it is coated with oil and nicely charred.
5. Add the cooked egg back into the wok and break into smaller pieces while you combine with the rice. If some of the rice sticks to the wok, don't worry as you can scrape it off easily and creates a

nice char taste (it happens when the oil was not enough).

6. Season with salt and white pepper. You can add more later after adding soy sauce, if not enough.

7. Add the soy sauce. The key action here is to toss the fried rice in the wok and make it fluffy instead of a big mess of fried rice sitting at the bottom of the wok.

8. Add green parts of the chopped green onion. And after tossing a few more times, transfer to a plate.

9. Fried rice at Chinese restaurants in Japan is often served in a dome shape. If you like to serve it this way, fill the fried rice in a rice bowl, pat down lightly to compact and invert onto a plate.

10. Sprinkle green onion on top, and serve!

Takikomi Gohan (Japanese Mixed Rice)

Takikomi Gohan is a wonderful and comforting Japanese mixed rice recipe made with seasonal ingredients. This recipe is also gluten free!

 PREP TIME: 20 Minutes   **COOK TIME:** 1 Hour   4 Servings

Ingredients

2 rice cooker cups **uncooked Japanese shortgrain rice** (1 ½ cup, 360 ml)

3 **dried shiitake mushrooms** (15 g)

½ cup **water** (120 ml)

⅓ package **konnyaku (konjac)** (3 oz, 85 g)

1 piece **aburaage (deepfried tofu pouch)** (¾ oz, 20 g)

2 oz **carrot** (3", 7.5 cm, 60 g)

1 oz **gobo (burdock root)** (4", 10 cm, 35 g)

1 **boneless, skinless chicken thigh** (4.8 oz, 135 g)

1 ½ cup **dashi** (Japanese soup stock) (360 ml)

Instructions

1. Wash the rice in a large bowl. Rice absorbs water very quickly when you start washing, so don't let the rice absorb the opaque water. Gently wash the rice in a circular motion and discard the water. Repeat this process about 3-4 times.

2. Let the rice soak in water for 30-60 minutes. This helps the rice absorb the seasonings later on and become more tender and moist after cooking. Transfer the rice into a sieve and drain completely for at least 15 minutes. Place the washed and drained rice in the rice cooker.

3. Meanwhile, prepare the other ingredients. Soak 3 dried shiitake mushrooms in a ½ cup of water for 15 minutes. I place a smaller bowl on top to keep the mushrooms submerged in the water at all times.

4. In a small saucepan, bring 2 cups of water to boil. Put ⅓ of the konnyaku and cook for 1 minute to get rid of the smell. Transfer the konnyaku to a plate to cool. Add the aburaage to the same pot of water and cook for 1 minute. This removes excess oil from the aburaage. Transfer aburaage to a plate to cool. Discard the water.

5. Shave off the gobo skin with the back of the knife. Don't peel the gobo with a peeler to keep the earthy flavor and fragrance. Then make a "cross" slit on tip of the gobo.

6. Make a lengthwise cross-shaped incision about 1 ½ inch deep at one end. Shave from that end as if you were sharpening a pencil with a knife while constantly rotating with the other hand. Soak in the water to prevent from changing color.

7. Cut the carrot in half lengthwise and cut diagonally into thin slices. Then cut the slices into julienned or smaller pieces.

8. Cut the aburaage and konnyaku into thin small strips.

9. Cut the chicken thigh into ¾ inch (2 cm) slanted pieces. Hold your knife at 45° angle and slice the chicken. This "sogigiri" cutting technique gives the chicken more surface area so it will cook faster and soak up flavors quickly.

1 ½ Tbsp **mirin**

1 ½ Tbsp **soy sauce**

mitsuba (Japanese parsley) (or 1 green onion)

10. Squeeze the liquid from dried shiitake mushrooms and save the liquid (this is called shiitake dashi). Remove the stem and cut the caps into thin slices.

11. Strain the shiitake dashi into a bowl through a fine mesh strainer to get rid of dirty particles. Set aside. In a measuring cup, add all the shiitake dashi and then pour dashi so you'll have 1 ½ cup (360ml) of liquid. Add it to the rice cooker and mix well.

12. Now your ingredients are ready!

13. Add 1 ½ Tbsp soy sauce and 1 ½ Tbsp mirin to the rice.

14. Pour the dashi & shiitake dashi mixture into the rice and mix well.

15. Add the chicken and evenly distribute over the rice. Do NOT mix the rice with ingredients. The rice won't be able to absorb enough water to cook and it will end up with a hard texture. Continue from the dense ingredients to softer ingredients. Without mixing all up, start cooking the rice. If you have a "Mixed Rice" option, use it.

16. Once the rice is done cooking, use a rice paddle to stir the rice and vegetables with light slicing and tossing motions to distribute the ingredients evenly. The bottom of the rice gets slightly caramelized, and this part is called *okoge* and it's especially tasty.

17. Serve the rice hot or at room temperature. Sprinkle chopped mitsuba or green onion on top. You can keep the leftover rice in the freezer for up to 1 month.

Onigiri (Japanese Rice Balls)

Stuffed with a variety of fillings and flavors, these rice balls make an ideal quick snack and are a fun alternative to sandwiches for lunch. In this recipe, you'll learn how to make onigiri using the common ingredients for rice balls in Japan.

 PREP TIME: 30 Minutes   **COOK TIME:** 30 Minutes   Servings: 12 Onigiri

Ingredients

FOR STEAMED RICE
2 cups uncooked **Japanese short-grain rice**

2 ½ cups **Water**

FOR MAKING ONIGIRI
kosher/sea salt (I use Diamond Crystal; Use half for table salt)

4 sheets **nori (seaweed)**

salted salmon

okaka

tuna mayo

3 **umeboshi (Japanese pickled plum)**(store bought)

seasoned kombu (store bought)

toasted white and black sesame seeds (to garnish)

Instructions

TO PREPARE ONIGIRI FILLINGS
1. While rice is being soaked and drained (45 minutes), prepare the onigiri fillings. Salted salmon filling: Sprinkle kosher salt on both sides of the salmon fillet. Bake at 400°F (200°C) degrees in an oven for 25 minutes.
2. Break the cooked salmon into flakes and set aside.
3. Umeboshi filling: Place umeboshi (Japanese pickled plums) on a 10" x 10" sheet of plastic wrap. Fold in half and squeeze the seed out from each umeboshi. Discard the seeds and keep the umeboshi flesh.
4. Okaka filling: Put katsuobushi (dried bonito flakes) in a bowl and add 2 Tbsp soy sauce. Mix to combine. Katsuobushi should be moistened but not drenched in soy sauce.
5. Tuna mayo filling: Put drained canned tuna in a bowl and add 2 Tbsp Japanese mayonnaise and ½ Tbsp soy sauce. Mix to combine.
6. Seasoned kombu filling: Put the purchased seasoned kombu in a bowl for easy access later.

TO MAKE ONIGIRI
1. Cut the nori sheets in thirds (⅓).
2. First, wet both of your hands with water so the rice won't stick.
3. Then put some salt in your hands and rub to spread all around your palms. How much salt? I dip 3 finger tips in kosher salt. If you are using table salt, use half amount as it's saltier than kosher salt.
4. Scoop out a handful of warm rice (about ⅓ cup) into one

FOR SALTED SALMON
1 fillet **salmon**

kosher/sea salt (I use Diamond Crystal; Use half for table salt)

FOR OKAKA
⅔ cup **katsuobushi (dried bonito flakes)** (6 g)

2 Tbsp **soy sauce**

FOR TUNA MAYO
1 **canned tuna** (2.5 oz = 70 g)

2 Tbsp **Japanese mayonnaise**

½ Tbsp **soy sauce**

hand. Create a small well (indentation) in the center of the rice. Put one kind of filling (about 1-2 tsp.) inside. Then mold the rice with your hands around the well to cover your filling completely.

5.   Press the rice around the filling to gently form the rice into a triangle. I use three fingers (thumb, index finger, middle finger) to make a triangle corner. Your hands should be just firm enough so the onigiri doesn't fall apart. You don't want to squeeze the rice too tight.

6.   Wrap the onigiri with nori (seaweed).

7.   Place a little bit of each filling on top of onigiri so we can tell them apart.

ALTERNATIVE METHOD OF MAKING ONIGIRI

1.   If you do not want to touch the rice at all, you can place a piece of plastic wrap in a rice bowl (or any small bowl) and put the rice on top. Sprinkle some kosher salt (salt is used to preserve the rice for a long time).

2.   Pull the plastic wrap corners and twist a few times.

3.   Form into a triangle shape with the same manner as I described above.

Yaki Onigiri (Grilled Rice Ball)

A favorite at Izakaya restaurants, Yaki Onigiri are Japanese grilled rice balls covered in savory soy sauce. With a crispy crust on the outside and soft sticky rice on the inside, these rice balls are simply irresistible and easy to make at home!

 PREP TIME: 15 Minutes   **COOK TIME:** 15 Minutes   Servings: 6 grilled rice balls

Ingredients

2 rice cooker cups **uncooked Japanese shortgrain rice** (360ml; 1 rice cooker cup (180ml) of uncooked rice will make 3 rice balls.)

kosher/sea salt (I use Diamond Crystal; Use half for table salt)

neutral-flavored oil (vegetable, canola, etc)

soy sauce (I used Homemade Unagi Sauce - recipe on page 270)

Instructions

1. Cook the rice in the rice cooker, pot over the stove top or pressure cooker.
2. Let the cooked rice cool a little bit until you can hold rice without burning your hands. Do not let the rice completely cool down.
3. First wet both of your hands with water so the rice won't stick. Make onigiri into triangle shapes.
4. Then put some salt in your hands and rub to spread all around.
5. Scoop about a half cup of rice onto your palm.
6. Cover the rice with the other hand and gently form the rice into a triangle.
7. Make sure the covering hand (for me it's my right hand) should be forming a triangle shape. Your hands should be just firm enough so the onigiri doesn't fall apart. You don't want to squeeze the rice too tight.
8. I use three fingers (thumb, index finger, middle finger) to cover the area to make a nice triangle shape. Then rotate onigiri to make a perfect triangle.
9. While you squeeze onigiri firmly with both hands, one of your hands has to press onigiri to keep a nice form.
10. Gently squeeze the center of triangle on both sides so there is a slight indentation (for grilling onigiri). Now onigiri is ready!
11. Lightly oil a cast iron skillet and put it on medium heat.
12. Grill onigiri until all sides are crispy and lightly browned. Don't flip it quickly. Just work on one side at a time and avoid turning over frequently.
13. Lower heat to medium low and brush all sides with soy sauce. Rotate to make sure all sides become crispy. Be careful not to burn onigiri after you brush it with the sauce.

TO STORE

Rice harden when you refrigerate. You can individually wrap the Yaki Onigiri in plastic wrap and cover them with a kitchen towel and store in the refrigerator for up to 2 days. The towel will prevent the rice from getting too cold. When you're ready to eat, bring it back to room temperature and reheat in microwave or frying pan.

NOODLES

Hot Soba Noodles

Topped with crispy shrimp tempura, fish cake and sliced scallion, this steamy bowl of Soba Noodle Soup is one of my favorite dishes to enjoy on the New Year's Eve. In Japan, it is a tradition to eat soba noodles on this day.

 PREP TIME: 15 Minutes   **COOK TIME:** 30 Minutes   2 Servings

Ingredients

4 cups **water** (4 cups = 960 ml)

1 piece **kombu (dried kelp)** (3" x 3" = 10 cm x 10 cm)

1 cup **katsuobushi (dried bonito flakes)** (10 g)

2 Tbsp **mirin**

1 Tbsp **sake**

2 Tbsp **soy sauce**

1 tsp **kosher/sea salt** (I use Diamond Crystal; Use half for table salt)

7 oz **dried soba noodles (buckwheat noodles)** (200 g)

TOPPINGS
4 slices **Kamaboko (fish cake)**

2 **frozen shrimp tempura**

1 **bunch komatsuna (or spinach)** (57 g)

Instructions

1. Soak kombu in water overnight or at least 30 minutes.
2. Transfer kombu and water into a saucepan. Bring the water to a boil. When it's almost boiling, remove kombu from water and discard.
3. Add katsuobushi and simmer for 30 seconds. Then turn off the heat and let katsuobushi sink to the bottom of pan. Let katsuobushi steep for about 10 minutes.
4. Strain the dashi over a large strainer lined with a paper towel set over another saucepan. Gently twist and squeeze the paper towel to release any remaining dashi into the saucepan.
5. Add mirin, sake, soy sauce, and salt in the dashi and bring the soup to a boil. Set aside until later.
6. Insert a knife at the bottom of kamaboko to separate it from the wooden board. Then cut the kamaboko into ¼" slices.
7. Slice green onion thinly and cut komatsuna into 2-inch pieces.
8. Boil the komatsuna in salted water. I first boil the hard bottom parts of komatsuna for 30 seconds since they take longer to cook. Then add the leafy part later. Once they are tender, take them out and soak in ice water to stop cooking. Drain well.
9. Bake shrimp tempura at 400°F (200°C) for 15 minutes, or according to the package instructions.
10. Meanwhile, boil two large pots of water. One for cooking soba noodles and the other pot for warming up the noodles after washing them. Cook soba 30 seconds less than the package instructions. Mine says cook for 4 minutes, so I cook for 3 minutes and 30 seconds. Unlike pasta, you do not

1 **green onion/scallion (or Tokyo negi)** (1 scallion = 3" Tokyo negi)

shichimi togarashi (Japanese seven spice) (or Ichimi Togarashi)

need to add salt to the water.

11. Drain the soba noodles and rinse under cold water to get rid of slimy texture.

12. Then transfer the soba noodles into the other pot of boiling water to warm up the noodles again. Once they are warm, drain and place them into a serving bowl.

13. Pour hot soup over the noodles and place toppings. Sprinkle shichimi togarashi or ichimi togarashi if you like it spicy. Serve immediately.

Zaru Soba (Cold Soba Noodles)

Light and refreshing, Zaru Soba (Cold Soba Noodles) will be your summer go-to staple. 10-minute is all you need to whip up this delicious noodle dish.

 PREP TIME: 5 Minutes   **COOK TIME:** 10 Minutes   4 Servings

Ingredients

14 oz **dried soba noodles (buckwheat noodles)** (400 g; 1 serving is 3.5 oz or 100 g)

1 part **mentsuyu/tsuyu (noodle soup base)**

1 part **iced water**

MENTSUYU (NOODLE SOUP BASE/DIPPING SAUCE): MAKES 1 CUP <u>CONCENTRATED</u> SAUCE
¼ cup **sake** (60 ml)

½ cup **mirin** (120 ml; I usually add additional 1 Tbsp)

½ cup **soy sauce** (120 ml)

1 **kombu (dried kelp)** (1" x 1" OR 2.5 cm x 2.5 cm)

1 cup **katsuobushi (dried bonito flakes)** (10 g)

TOPPINGS/GARNISH
shredded nori seaweed

Instructions

TO MAKE DIPPING SAUCE (MAKES 1 CUP <u>CONCENTRATED</u> SAUCE):

1. In a medium saucepan, add ¼ cup sake and bring it to a boil over medium-high heat. Let the alcohol evaporate for a few seconds.
2. Add ½ cup soy sauce and ½ cup mirin.
3. Add 1 x 1 inch (2.5 x 2.5 cm) kombu and 1 cup dried bonito flakes (katsuobushi).
4. Bring it to a boil and cook on low heat for 5 minutes. Turn off the heat and set aside until it cools down. Strain the sauce and set aside. You can keep the sauce in an airtight container and store in the refrigerator for up to a month.

TO BOIL SOBA NOODLES:

1. Boil a lot of water in a large pot. Unlike with boiling pasta, you DO NOT add salt to the water. Add dried soba noodles in the boiling water in a circular motion, separating the noodles from each other.
2. Cook soba noodles according to the package instructions (each brand is slightly different). Stir the noodles once in a while so they don't stick to each other. Check the tenderness and do not overcook. Before you drain, reserve 1 to 1 ½ cup of soba cooking water, "sobayu".
3. Drain the soba noodles into the sieve and rinse the noodles to get rid of starch under running cold water. **IMPORTANT**
4. Shake off the sieve to drain completely and transfer the noodles to the iced water in a large bowl. Set aside until the noodles are cool.
5. To serve the noodles, place a bamboo sieve or mat over a plate (to catch water from noodles). Put soba noodles and garnish with shredded nori sheet on top.

(kizami nori)

2 **green onions/scallions**

wasabi (optional)

TO SERVE:
1. To make the dipping sauce, combine 1 part of cooled dipping sauce and 3 parts of iced water in a serving pitcher or small individual bowls (sauce: water = 1:3). Check the taste. If it's salty, add more water. If it's diluted, add more sauce.
2. Put chopped green onions and wasabi on a small plate and serve with the soba noodles.

Miso Ramen

You can make delicious Miso Ramen with authentic broth in less than 30 minutes! Please note: toppings are optional and their recipes can be found in the hyperlinks. Chashu and Ramen Eggs require to prep one day before.

 PREP TIME: 10 Minutes   **COOK TIME:** 15 Minutes   2 Servings

Ingredients

FOR RAMEN SOUP:
2 cloves **garlic** (1 ½ tsp minced garlic)

1 knob **ginger** (½ tsp grated ginger)

1 **shallot**

1 Tbsp **toasted white sesame seeds**

1 Tbsp **sesame oil** (roasted)

¼ lb **ground pork** (113 g)

1 tsp **doubanjiang (spicy chili bean sauce/broad bean paste)** (You can buy nonspicy version online.)

3 Tbsp **miso** (Each miso brand/type makes slightly different broth)

1 Tbsp **sugar**

1 Tbsp **sake**

4 cups **chicken stock/broth** (960 ml; each ramen bowl requires about 1 ½ cup (355 ml) of broth + a bit more for evaporation)

Instructions

TO PREPARE RAMEN SOUP
1. Mince the garlic (I use a garlic press) and ginger (I use a ceramic grater).
2. Mince the shallot.
3. Grind sesame seeds, leaving some seeds unground for texture.
4. In a medium pot, heat sesame oil over medium-low and add the minced garlic, ginger, and shallot.
5. With a wooden spatula, stir fry until fragrant.
6. Add the meat and increase heat to medium. Cook the meat until no longer pink.
7. Add spicy bean paste (La Doubanjiang) or non-spicy bean paste (Doubanjiang) and miso. Quickly blend well with the meat before they get burnt.
8. And add the ground sesame seeds and sugar and mix well.
9. Add sake and chicken stock, and bring it to a simmer.
10. Taste your soup and add salt (if necessary) and white pepper. Each chicken stock brand varies in saltiness, so taste and season accordingly.
11. Cover with the lid and keep the ramen soup simmered while you cook the noodles.

TO PREPARE TOPPINGS AND NOODLES
1. Bring a large pot of unsalted water to a boil (ramen noodles already contain salt). When water is boiling, place some hot water into serving bowls to warm up the bowls (and drain before adding cooked noodles). Loosen up the fresh noodles.

1 tsp **kosher/sea salt** (I use Diamond Crystal; Use half for table salt) (adjust according to your chicken broth)

¼ tsp **white pepper powder**

FOR RAMEN & OPTIONAL TOPPINGS:
2 servings ramen noodles (10-12 oz or 283-340 g fresh noodles; 6.3 oz or 180 g dry ramen noodles)

chashu (recipe page 136)

spicy bean sprout salad (or blanched bean sprout)

ramen eggs (recipe page 90)

corn kernels (drained)

nori (seaweed) (cut a sheet into quarters)

green onion/scallion (chopped)

shiraga negi (recipe page 280)

FOR RAMEN & OPTIONAL TOPPINGS:

la-yu (Japanese chili oil)

pickled red ginger (beni shoga or kizami beni shoga)

white pepper powder

2. **Important:** Prepare ramen toppings ahead of time so you can serve ramen hot immediately. For toppings, I usually put chashu, ramen egg, blanched bean sprout, corn kernels, shiraga negi, chopped green onion, and a sheet of nori. Prepare a small dish of red pickled ginger, la-yu (chili oil), and white pepper powder on the table.
3. Cook the noodles according to the package instructions. I usually cook the noodles al dente (about 15 seconds earlier than suggested time).
4. When noodles are done, quickly pick them up with a mesh sieve. You don't want to dilute your soup, so make sure to drain the water well. Serve the noodles into bowls.
5. Add the ramen soup and top with various toppings you've prepared.
6. Place the toppings of your choice and serve immediately.

Yakisoba

Yakisoba is a classic Japanese stir fry noodles dish with pork and vegetables, and it's seasoned with a sweet & savory sauce similar to Worcestershire sauce.

 PREP TIME: 10 Minutes   **COOK TIME:** 20 Minutes   3 Servings

Ingredients

½ **onion**

1 **carrot**

3 **shiitake mushrooms**

2 **green onions/scallions**

4 cabbage leaves

¾ lb **sliced pork belly** (340 g; or your choice of meat and/or seafood)

2 Tbsp **neutral-flavored oil** (vegetable, canola, etc)

freshly ground black pepper

1 package **yakisoba noodles** (one package comes with 3 servings, 16- 17 oz or 454-480 g)

4-6 Tbsp **yakisoba sauce**

YAKISOBA SAUCE (MAKES ½ CUP (8 TBSP))
4 Tbsp **Worcestershire sauce** (Japanese brand "Bulldog" Worcestershire sauce (Usuta-so-su, ウスターソース) is milder and less sour than Lea & Perrins Worcestershire sauce.

4 tsp **oyster sauce** (If you're allergic to shellfish,

Instructions

TO MAKE YAKISOBA SAUCE

1. Whisk all the ingredients for yakisoba sauce. It's important to taste the sauce and see if you need to add more sugar (For example, some ketchup is sweeter than others while some Worcestershire sauce is less sour than others). Set aside.

TO MAKE YAKISOBA

1. Slice the onion, cut the carrot into julienned strips, and slice the shiitake mushrooms.
2. Chop the green onion into 2-inch pieces, cut the cabbage into small-bite pieces, and cut the meat into 1-inch pieces.
3. In a skillet or wok, heat oil on medium-high. Cook the meat until no longer pink.
4. Add the onion and carrot and cook for 1-2 minutes.
5. Add the cabbage and cook until almost tender.
6. Lastly, add the green onion and shiitake mushrooms and cook for 1 minute. Season with freshly ground black pepper.
7. Transfer the yakisoba noodles to a sieve and quickly run hot water over yakisoba noodle. Separate the noodles with hands. Add the noodles to the skillet/ wok, and lower the heat to medium.

use LEE KUM KEE Vegetarian Stir-Fry Sauce)

4 tsp **ketchup**

2 tsp **soy sauce**

2 tsp **sugar** (Add more if needed)

TOPPINGS (OPTIONAL)
Aonori (dried green seaweed)

pickled red ginger (beni shoga or kizami beni shoga)

It's best to use tongs to combine the noodles with ingredients. Keep an eye on the noodles as they may stick to the skillet/wok.

8. Add Yakisoba Sauce. Depending on the amount of ingredients, adjust the amount of sauce to use. Mix all together using tongs. Transfer to plates and garnish with dried green seaweed and pickled red ginger. Serve immediately.

Yaki Udon (Stir-Fried Udon Noodles)

Yaki Udon is Japanese stir-fried udon noodles made with your choice of protein and vegetables seasoned with a savory sauce. Ready in 25 mins, and incredibly delicious!

 PREP TIME: 10 Minutes   **COOK TIME:** 15 Minutes   2 Servings

Ingredients

2 servings **udon noodles** (180 g dry udon noodles; 500 g frozen/boiled udon noodles)

½ **onion**

2-3 leaves **cabbage**

1 **carrot**

2 **shiitake mushrooms**

2 **green onions/scallions**

½ lb **sliced pork belly** (227 g: or your choice of meat, seafood, or extra vegetables/mushrooms)

1 Tbsp **neutral-flavored oil** (vegetable, canola, etc)

SEASONINGS
freshly ground black pepper

3 Tbsp **mentsuyu/tsuyu (noodle soup base)** (mentsuyu I use is 3-times concentrated. If you use non-concentrated Mentsuyu, you might need to add more to achieve the same flavor. You could skip Mentsuyu and

Instructions

1. I like using frozen Sanuki udon noodles, which require boiling for just 1 minute before using (no need to defrost). If you use dried udon noodles, boil them according to the package instructions.
2. Bring a large pot of water to a boil and cook the udon noodles.
3. Slice onion and cut cabbage into 1" (2.5 cm) square pieces. Julienne the carrot (cut into 2" (5 cm) matchsticks).
4. Discard the tough shiitake stems and slice the mushroom tops. Thinly slice the top 2" (5 cm) green part of scallions and set aside (for garnish). Cut the rest of scallion into 2" (5 cm) pieces.
5. Cut the pork belly slices into 1" (2.5 cm) pieces.
6. In a frying pan, heat oil over medium-high. Add the pork and cook until almost cooked through. Then add onion and cook until translucent and soft.
7. Add cabbage and carrots and stir fry until coated with oil. Then add shiitake mushrooms and scallion. Stir fry until vegetables are lightly wilted.
8. Add udon noodles and using tongs, combine well with all the ingredients.
9. Add seasonings (Freshly ground black pepper, 3 Tbsp mentsuyu, and 1 tsp soy sauce) and mix all together. Adjust the amount of mentsuyu based on the amount of the ingredients you have added.
10. Serve on a plate and sprinkle bonito flakes and green onions on top. Garnish with red pickled

increase the soy sauce to a total of 2-3 Tbsp (gradually increase, please), but the final dish will taste slightly different.)

1 tsp **soy sauce**

TOPPINGS
3 Tbsp **katsuobushi (dried bonito flakes)** (or 1 small package of katsuobushi)

1 Tbsp **pickled red ginger** (beni shoga or kizami beni shoga) (optional)

ginger on the side if you like.

Curry Udon

Thick chewy udon noodles soaked in a rich, fragrant curry sauce! This Curry Udon will satisfy your noodles craving in an instant. Bonus: it's simple enough to throw together on a busy weeknight.

 PREP TIME: 10 Minutes   **COOK TIME:** 40 Minutes   2 Servings

Ingredients

½ **onion** (5.7 oz or 162 g)

2 **green onions/scallions** (finely chopped)

1 Tbsp **neutral-flavored oil** (vegetable, canola, etc)

6 oz **thinly sliced pork loin** (170 g; Or use your choice of protein; cut into small pieces)

1 Tbsp **sake**

3 cups **dashi** (Japanese soup stock) (720 ml)

2 cubes **Japanese curry roux** (Roughly 2 oz or 50 g total. You can make homemade Japanese curry roux.)

2 tsp **soy sauce**

2 servings **udon noodles** (6.3 oz/180 g dry udon noodles; 1.1 lb/500 g frozen/boiled udon noodles)

Instructions

1. You will need to break the curry roux into cubes and use 2 pieces. Prepare dashi with your preferred method, if you haven't any.
2. Thinly slice the onion and green onions.
3. In a medium pot, heat oil on medium heat and add the onion.
4. Sauté the onion for 2-3 minutes, and then add the meat.
5. Cook the meat until almost no longer pink and add sake.
6. Add dashi and cover with the lid. Reduce the heat to medium-low and cook for 5 minutes.
7. When simmering, skim off the scum and fat from the stock and continue to cook.
8. Meanwhile, start boiling a separate large pot of water for udon.
9. After 5 minutes, turn off the heat for the medium sauce pot. Add a curry roux cube in a ladle, let it dissolve one cube at a time (We'll use 2 cubes in total).
10. Using chopsticks or spoon, let the roux dissolve completely in a ladle, before releasing it to the soup. *Tip: Take time to dissolve the roux completely.*
11. Add soy sauce and mix well. Turn off the heat and cover the lid to keep it warm.
12. When the water is boiling, cook your udon noodles according to the package instruction.
13. Drain the noodles and divide into two bowls. Pour the curry over the udon noodles. Top with green onion and serve immediately.

Beef Udon (Niku Udon)

Craving for a steamy bowl of hot noodle soup? This Beef Udon, my-go-to Japanese comfort dish is absolutely heart-warming. Tender sliced beef on top of slippery warm udon noodle in a savory broth. What's not to love?

 PREP TIME: 10 Minutes    **COOK TIME:** 15 Minutes    2 Servings

Ingredients

1 Tbsp **neutral-flavored oil** (vegetable, canola, etc)

½ **negi (long green onion)** (Sub: ½ leek or 2 scallions/green onions)

½ lb **thinly sliced beef** (chuck or rib eye) (227 g) (ribeye or top sirloin)

2 servings **udon noodles** (180 g dry udon noodles; 500 g frozen/boiled udon noodles)

FOR BEEF
1 Tbsp **soy sauce**

½-1 Tbsp **sugar**

FOR SOUP
2 cups **dashi** (Japanese soup stock) (480 ml)

1 Tbsp **soy sauce**

1 Tbsp **mirin**

1 tsp **sugar**

pinch **kosher/sea salt** (I use

Instructions

1. In a small saucepan, add 2 cups (480 ml) dashi and 1 tsp sugar.
2. Add 1 Tbsp mirin and 1 Tbsp soy sauce and bring it to a boil.
3. Taste the soup and adjust the taste with kosher salt as it will enhance the flavor. Cover and keep it on low heat.
4. Cut the Tokyo negi and narutomaki (fish cake) diagonally.
5. Cut the mitsuba (optional) into small pieces and thinly slice one onion/scallion (used for topping).
6. Cut the thinly sliced meat into bite-size pieces.
7. Bring a large pot of water to a boil for udon noodles. My favorite udon is the frozen Sanuki Udon. Cook the frozen udon noodles in boiling water for 1 minute (no need to defrost). If you use dry noodles, follow the package instructions.
8. Once the udon is done cooking, drain water and transfer to serving bowls.
9. While cooking udon, you can start heating the large frying pan. Once it's heated, add 1 Tbsp vegetable oil and cook the negi until tender.
10. Add the meat and brown on all sides. Don't move the meat around until it's nicely seared.
11. Once the meat is nicely browned, add ½ to 1 Tbsp sugar and 1 Tbsp soy sauce. When the sauce has caramelized and slightly thickened, turn off the heat.
12. By this time, the noodle should be in the serving bowls. Pour the hot soup over the udon noodles in the

Diamond Crystal; Use half for table salt)

FOR TOPPINGS
narutomaki (fish cakes) (6 slices)

3 **sprigs mitsuba (Japanese parsley)** (Optional)

1 **green onion/scallion**

shichimi togarashi (Japanese seven spice) (for taste)

bowls. Then serve the meat on top of the udon noodles.

13. Place the narutomaki (fish cake) and garnish with scallion and mitsuba. If you like it spicy, sprinkle shichimi togarashi (Japanese 7 spice). Enjoy!

Miso Butter Pasta with Tuna and Cabbage

With al-dente spaghetti tossed in delicious Japanese-style seasoning, this Miso Butter Pasta with Tuna and Cabbage makes a quick meal you'll love. It takes only simple pantry ingredients and ready in 15 minutes!

 PREP TIME: 5 Minutes   **COOK TIME:** 10 Minutes   2 Servings

Ingredients

1 Tbsp **kosher/sea salt** (I use Diamond Crystal; Use half for table salt) (for cooking pasta)

7 oz **spaghetti** (200 g)

2 cloves **garlic**

3 leaves **cabbage** (5 oz, 142 g)

1 can **canned tuna** (2.8 oz, 80g)

1 Tbsp **extra-virgin olive oil**

freshly ground black pepper

1 Tbsp **unsalted butter** (14 g)

1 Tbsp **miso**

4 Tbsp **reserved pasta water** (¼ cup, 60 ml)

2 tsp **soy sauce**

2 tsp **mirin**

Instructions

TO COOK SPAGHETTI

1. Start boiling 4 quarts (16 cups, 3.8 L) water in a large pot (I used a 4.5 QT Dutch oven). Once boiling, add salt and spaghetti.
2. Stir to make sure spaghetti doesn't stick to each other. *Tip: I usually reduce the cooking time by 1 minute if I have to continue cooking the pasta afterward. Drain if you finish cooking the spaghetti first, but you should be able to cook the rest of the ingredients in 10 minutes while spaghetti is being cooked.*

TO PREPARE INGREDIENTS

1. While cooking pasta, prepare the ingredients. Peel the garlic cloves and thinly slice them.
2. Remove the tough core of the cabbage and cut into 1-inch square pieces.
3. Drain the canned tuna. If you use a big chunk, you can break into smaller pieces (optional).

TO COOK TUNA AND CABBAGE JAPANESE PASTA

1. Heat the olive oil in a large frying pan over medium heat. Add the garlic to the pan immediately to start infusing the oil. Make sure to coat well.
2. When the garlic is sizzling and well-coated with oil, add the cabbage and coat with the oil for 2 minutes or so.
3. Add the canned tuna and toss it together with the cabbage.
4. Add freshly ground black pepper, unsalted butter, and miso. Stir to mix well and let the butter melt completely.
5. Reserve 4 Tbsp (¼ cup, 60 ml) of pasta water and add to the

frying pan.

6. Shake the pan and mix all the ingredients together. Make sure the miso is dissolved while mixing by this time.

7. Add the soy sauce and mirin.

8. When the spaghetti is done cooking, pick up the noodles with a pair of tongs (or you can quickly drain in the sink) and add to the pan. Toss the spaghetti to mix all together.

9. Season the spaghetti with freshly ground pepper. Taste and add salt if needed. Serve the pasta in individual dishes. Enjoy!

Japanese Pasta with Shrimp and Asparagus

Seasoned with soy sauce and flavorful dashi broth, this Japanese-style Pasta with Shrimp and Asparagus is incredibly delicious and ready in less than 30 minutes!

 PREP TIME: 10 Minutes   **COOK TIME:** 20 Minutes   2 Servings

Ingredients

¼ **red onion** (2.5 oz, 70 g)

2 cloves **garlic**

6 oz **asparagus** (170 g)

10 **large shrimp** (peeled and deveined; 9 oz, 260 g)

kosher/sea salt (I use Diamond Crystal; Use half for table salt)

freshly ground black pepper

1 Tbsp **extra-virgin olive oil**

1 ½-2 Tbsp **unsalted butter** (21-28 g)

1-2 **dried red chili pepper** (seeds removed; optional)

¼-⅓ cup **dashi** (Japanese soup stock) (60-80 ml)

1 Tbsp **soy sauce**

crushed red peppers (red

Instructions

1. Bring a big pot of water to a boil.
2. Meanwhile, cut red onion and garlic cloves into thin slices.
3. Cut asparagus diagonally and separate spears and stalks; we will sauté asparagus stalks first as they take longer to cook.
4. Sprinkle kosher salt and freshly ground black pepper on shrimp.
5. Once the pasta water is boiling, for 4QT (16 cups or 3.8L) add 2 Tbsp salt. As we will cook the pasta a little longer after draining, cook it 1 minute less than the directions on the package.
6. Heat 1 Tbsp olive oil in a large skillet over medium heat. When it's hot, add shrimp and cook until the bottom side is nicely browned, about 2-3 minutes. Don't touch the shrimp until it releases itself from the skillet. Once it has nice char on one side, you can easily flip.
7. When the one side of the shrimp is nicely browned, flip and cook the other side for 2-3 minutes. Once the shrimp are nicely golden brown, transfer to a plate and set aside.
8. Lower the heat to medium-low, add the butter, and swirl around.
9. Add the red onion and garlic slices and sauté for 1 minute. If you like spicy pasta, add chili pepper now. Increase the heat to medium and add the stalks of asparagus. Sauté for about 3 minutes, or until tender.
10. Then add asparagus spears and cook for another 1-2 minutes until tender but still nice and crisp.
11. Add the shrimp back into the skillet and increase the heat to medium-high. Add dashi.
12. Add soy sauce and adjust based on your preference.
13. Add the cooked pasta and toss to combine with the ingredi-

pepper flakes) (optional)

8 oz **pasta** (226 g)

ents. If you like, sprinkle freshly ground black pepper. Serve immediately. Garnish with chili pepper flakes (Optional).

Ume Shisho Pasta

If you enjoy Japanese style (wafu) pasta, you'd love this Ume Shiso Pasta where simple ingredients bring out the best of a dish.

 PREP TIME: 5 Minutes   **COOK TIME:** 15 Minutes   2 Servings

Ingredients

8 oz **spaghetti** (226 g)

10-20 **shiso leaves (perilla/ooba)** (I like to use a lot for more flavor)

2 cloves **garlic**

1.8 oz **shimeji mushrooms** (½ package, 50 g)

2 pieces **umeboshi (Japanese pickled plum)**

4 pieces **chicken tenders** (these are also known as chicken fingers and chicken strips. I like to use this part of chicken because they are moist when cooked. These strips of white meat are located on either side of the breastbone, under the breast meat (pectoralis major).)

¼ tsp **kosher/sea salt** (I use Diamond Crystal; use half for table salt)

freshly ground black pepper

Instructions

1. Cook spaghetti according to the package instruction in lightly salted boiling water. However, as we will be further cooking spaghetti with the sauce, cook about 1 minute less than the package instruction. Make sure to reserve ½ cup of pasta cooking water before you drain the spaghetti into a colander.
2. Meanwhile, roll up shiso leaves and julienne into thin strips.
3. Slice garlic and discard the bottom part of buna shimeji mushrooms.
4. Remove a seed from umeboshi and discard. Then mince into small pieces.
5. Slice the chicken tender diagonally into 1 inch (2.5 cm) pieces (this cutting technique is called "sogigiri") and season them with salt and pepper.
6. Sprinkle the flour over the chicken and coat it well with your hands.
7. Heat the olive oil on medium-high heat and cook garlic until fragrant.
8. Add the chicken and cook until no longer pink. Then cook the shimeji mushrooms till coated with oil.
9. Add half (¼ cup) of the reserved pasta cooking water, soy sauce, and umeboshi.
10. When the chicken is coated with the sauce, add the spaghetti into the pan.
11. Using a tong, coat the spaghetti well with the sauce. If you need more sauce, add the pasta cooking water and soy sauce and adjust the flavor. Season with salt and freshly ground black pepper to your taste .
12. Garnish with shiso leaves and shredded nori on top.

1 Tbsp **all-purpose flour** (plain flour) (7.5 g)

2 Tbsp **extra-virgin olive oil** (1 Tbsp for non stick pan)

1 Tbsp **soy sauce**

¼ cup **shredded nori seaweed** (kizami nori)

TO STORE

You can keep the leftovers in an airtight container and store in the refrigerator for up to 3 days and in the freezer for a month.

Macaroni Gratin

So amazingly rich, creamy, and buttery, this Macaroni Gratin with easy homemade white sauce is true comfort food! Guaranteed to be everyone's favorite meal for dinner.

 PREP TIME: 20 Minutes   **COOK TIME:** 50 Minutes   4 Servings

Ingredients

12 pieces **shrimp** (5 oz or 142 g)

2 **boneless, skinless chicken thighs** (227 g)

2 Tbsp **sake** (separated)

1 Tbsp **extra-virgin olive oil**

⅛ tsp **kosher/sea salt** (I use Diamond Crystal; Use half for table salt)

freshly ground black pepper

4 Tbsp **unsalted butter** (¼ cup or 56 g (Please do not reduce the amount))

½ **onion** (6 oz or 170 g)

6 **cremini mushrooms** or button mushrooms (4 oz or 113 g)

1 Tbsp **mirin**

6 Tbsp **all-purpose flour** (plain flour) (45 g)

Instructions

1. If your shrimp come with veins, peel the shell, remove the tail, and devein by scoring the back of shrimp and removing the black veins. Put the shrimp in a small bowl and add 1 Tbsp sake. Coat the shrimp well with sake to remove the smell.
2. Cut the chicken into small bite-size pieces, about 1-inch cubes. Put them in a small bowl and add 1 Tbsp sake to remove the smell.
3. Thinly slice the onion. Cut the mushrooms into ¼ inch thick slices.
4. Heat a large frying pan over medium heat and add 1 Tbsp olive oil. I use a 3.75QT braiser, which you can put in the oven and serve directly. Add the shrimp in a single layer.
5. Season with salt and black pepper and cook until the bottom side changes color.
6. Flip and cook the other side. When both sides achieve nice pink color, transfer to a plate. Do not overcook the shrimp. The remaining heat will continue to cook the shrimp, and later when the shrimp is cooked in the white sauce.
7. In the same pan, add the 4 Tbsp butter to the pan and let it melt over medium heat. You will need this much fat to make enough white sauce for your macaroni. Add the onion and sauté until it is coated with butter.
8. Add the chicken and cook, stirring occasionally, until no longer pink. Season with salt and black pepper.
9. When the chicken is no longer pink, add the mushrooms and coat with the oil.
10. Add the shrimp back into the pan. Add 1 Tbsp mirin to the mixture and quickly coat with the ingredients.
11. Turn the heat to medium-low and gradually add 6 Tbsp

2 ½ cups **whole milk** (600 ml)

½ cup **heavy whipping cream** (120 ml)

1 tsp **kosher/sea salt** (I use Diamond Crystal; Use half for table salt)

½ tsp **ground white pepper**

PASTA
8 oz **macaroni** (or elbow pasta - 227 g or 2 cups)

1 Tbsp **kosher/sea salt** (I use Diamond Crystal; Use half for table salt) (for cooking pasta in 3 QT water)

TOPPINGS
2 oz **Gruyere cheese** (50 g)

2 oz **Parmesan cheese** (50 g)

3 Tbsp **panko** (Japanese breadcrumbs)(11 g)

chives (to garnish)

all-purpose flour to the mixture, stirring to combine with the ingredients.

12. If the bottom of the pan is getting burnt, turn off the heat until you blend the flour with ingredients, then turn the heat back on to continue this process. Once the flour is well blended, cook for 2 minutes.

13. Then <u>gradually</u> add the milk, ¼ cup at a time.

14. Blend with the mixture well before you add the next ¼ cup of milk. The mixture will continue to thicken as you cook.

15. Once all the milk is incorporated, add heavy whipping cream and cook for 3-5 minutes, stirring frequently.

16. At this stage, you need to taste the white sauce and add salt and white pepper to taste. Remember to season a bit more than you would normally do. You will add in macaroni later, which makes the sauce less salty. Turn off the heat and set aside.

17. To cook the pasta, bring the water to a rolling boil. Stir in salt (I added 1 Tbsp salt to 3 qt of water). Then cook the pasta al dente according to the package directions. Drain well.

18. Stir the white sauce on medium-low heat and add the drained macaroni to combine with the sauce.

19. If you are using the oven-safe braiser, skip this step. If you are using individual gratin baking dishes, grease them with softened butter. Divide the macaroni mixture into 4 baking dishes.

20. Divide the mixture – each 6.5" baking dish should be filled to 90%.

21. Grate the Gruyère and Parmigiano Reggiano and generously sprinkle over the macaroni mixture.

22. Sprinkle panko on top of the cheese, a bit less than 1 Tbsp for each baking dish. Broil high for 3-5 minutes (depending on the distance from the heat source), or until golden brown. If you don't have a broiler, bake at preheated 450 °F (230 °C) oven for 15 minutes, or until golden brown.

23. When the cheese is melted and panko is nicely charred, remove from the oven. Sprinkle finely chopped chives and serve immediately.

SUSHI

How To Make Sushi Rice

Learn how to make sushi rice perfectly every time. All you need is simple ingredients such as sushi vinegar, sugar, salt and dashi kombu. Once you master the secret of making the rice, you will be ready to dish up all kinds of mouthwatering sushi recipes!

 PREP TIME: 10 Minutes   **COOK TIME:** 1 Hour   Servings: 6 cups

Ingredients

3 rice cooker cups **uncooked Japanese shortgrain rice** (540 ml, 3 gō, 3 合, 450 g)

540 ml **water**

2 inches **kombu (dried kelp)** (5 g, 2" x 2" OR 5 cm x 5 cm; optional - but it will give nice aroma!)

⅓ cup **rice vinegar** (80 ml)

HOMEMADE SUSHI VINEGAR
⅓ cup **rice vinegar** (80 ml)

3 Tbsp **sugar** (You can use 2 Tbsp if you want to cut down on sugar)

1 ½ tsp **kosher/sea salt** (I use Diamond Crystal; Use half for table salt)

Instructions

TO COOK RICE

1. Please note: 1 rice cooker cup is 180 ml. So when using a rice cooker, "a cup" means a <u>rice cooker cup</u>.
2. Put rice in a large bowl. Rinse the rice and discard the water immediately. Rice absorbs water very quickly when you start washing, so don't let the rice absorb the unclear water. Repeat this process 1-2 times.
3. Now use your fingers to gently wash the rice by moving in a circular motion.
4. Rinse and discard water. Repeat this process 3-4 times. Repeat the rinsing process 3-4 times until the water is almost clear.
5. Transfer the rice into a sieve and drain completely.
6. Gently clean the dashi kombu with a damp cloth (it's a traditional method, but these days kombu is much cleaner). Make sure not to wipe off the white powdery substances, which contribute to the umami flavor in dashi. NEVER wash the kombu.
7. Put the rice in the rice cooker bowl and add water (never hot or warm) to just under the 3-cup line. If your rice cooker has a "Sushi Rice" option, add water until that line. Place the kombu on top of the rice and let the rice soak in water for 20-30 minutes. *Tip: Since you add sushi vinegar to the cooked rice, the rice should be cooked on the firm side.* **If you cook rice on the stovetop, the water to rice ratio for sushi rice should be 1 to 1** (instead of 1 to 1.1 or 1 to 1.2 for regular steamed rice).

TO MAKE SUSHI VINEGAR

To make sushi vinegar, combine rice vinegar, sugar, and salt in a small saucepan and bring it to a boil over medium-high heat. Whisk until the sugar is completely dissolved. You can also put the

ingredients in a microwave-safe bowl and microwave for 1 minute, or till sugar is dissolved. Set aside to let it cool.

TO MAKE SUSHI RICE

1. When the rice is cooked, moisten sushi oke/hangiri (a round, flat-bottom wooden tub) or a baking sheet lined with parchment paper, or a large moisten glass bowl. Transfer the cooked rice into the sushi oke and spread out evenly so the rice will cool faster. While it's hot, pour sushi vinegar over the rice. *Tip: If you're making more/less rice or using the sushi vinegar bottle, the required sushi vinegar for rice should be roughly 8-10% of the cooked rice weight.*
2. With a rice paddle, slice the rice at a 45 degree angle to separate the chunks of rice instead of mixing. At the same time, you need to use a fan to cool rice so the rice will shine and doesn't get mushy.
3. Then gently flip the rice in between slices. Repeat this process until the rice is cooled to your skin temperature (about 91 °F/ 33 °C)..

TO KEEP

Keep the rice covered with a damp towel (or paper towel) at room temperature until ready to use.

Sushi Rolls (Maki Sushi – Hosomaki)

Learn how to make delicious sushi rolls - Maki Sushi (Hosomaki) at home. To get started, you just need a few ingredients like tuna, cucumber, nori, and Japanese short-grain rice.

 PREP TIME: 1 Hour   **COOK TIME:** 1 Hour   Servings: 10 sushi rolls

Ingredients

FOR SUSHI RICE
3 rice cooker cups **uncooked Japanese shortgrain rice** (540 ml, 450 g; you MUST use short-grain Japanese rice to make sushi. Otherwise, rice will fall apart.)

1 piece **kombu (dried kelp)** (2 x 2 inches or 5 x 5 cm)

540 ml **water**

⅓ cup **rice vinegar** (If you decide to use the convenient Sushi Vinegar (Seasoned Rice Vinegar), instead of making your own with rice vinegar, you do not need sugar and salt)(80 ml)

3 Tbsp **sugar**

1 ½ tsp **kosher/sea salt**

Instructions

Gather all the ingredients. Note: The cook time does not include time for cooking rice as it varies depending on the device/method. You will need a bamboo sushi mat.

TO PREPARE SUSHI RICE
1. 1 uncooked rice cooker cup (180 ml) will make 2 rice cooker cups of cooked rice. For this recipe, **2 cups of uncooked rice** (4 cups of cooked rice) will make **10 Hosomaki** (thin sushi rolls).
2. Please read sushi rice recipe. Cover the sushi rice and the completed rolls with a damp cloth/plastic wrap at all times to prevent from drying.

TO PREPARE THE FILLINGS
1. Cut both ends of the cucumber. Then cut in half lengthwise and cut again in half so you now have 4 strips. Remove the seeds with knife and cut in half lengthwise again. You should end up with 8 cucumber strips.
2. Cut the tuna into ¼- ½" slices and then cut into ¼- ½" thick long strips.
3. Take out the natto from the container and season with soy sauce or seasoning that came with the package. Mix everything up until it's slimy and bubbly.

TO ROLL SUSHI
1. Make vinegared hand-dipping water *(tezu)* by combining ¼ cup water and 1 Tbsp rice vinegar in a small bowl. Applying this water to your hands prevents the rice from sticking to your hands.
2. Cut nori in half. Nori sheets are not perfectly square; therefore cut the longer side of the rectangular in half. Also, nori gets stale easily,

(I use Diamond Crystal;
Use half for table salt)

FILLINGS OF YOUR CHOICE:

1 **Persian/Japanese cucumbe**r (yield 8 rolls)

7 oz **sashimi-grade tuna** (200 g) (yield 12 rolls)

1 box **natto (fermented soybean)** (yield 2 rolls)

TEZU (VINEGARED HANDDIPPING WATER):

¼ cup **water**

1 Tbsp **rice vinegar**

EVERYTHING ELSE:

5 sheets **nori (seaweed)**

soy sauce

wasabi (optional)

sushi ginger (optional)

so store unused nori in an air-tight bag and take out only as much as you need.

3. Place the sushi mat on a working surface. The bamboo strings should go sideways so you can roll them up. And put the halved nori sheet on the bamboo mat, with one of nori's long side close to the back edge of the mat. Leave about 3-4 slats visible on the side nearest to you. The shiny side of nori should face DOWN.

4. Moisten your hand before you touch the sushi rice.

5. Scoop a scant ½ cup of sushi rice into your hand. My trick is to use a ½ cup measuring cup. That way the amount of rice for each roll is the same and the rolls will be equal size. Make sure to wet the measuring cup so the rice won't stick.

6. Place the sushi rice on the left center of nori. Spread the rice across the nori, leaving a 1" space along the top edge of the nori. Use your right hand to spread the rice toward the right and use your left fingers to keep the rice away from the 1" space on the top of the nori.

7. Spread the rice evenly with both fingers, still keeping the 1" space on the top. Wet your fingers in dipping water if the rice starts to stick.

8. Place the filling (tuna, cucumber, natto) in the middle of the rice. If your tuna or cucumber is a bit too short, add extra pieces on the end. Hold the filling down using your fingers.

9. With one swift movement, roll the sushi over the filling and land right where the edge of the rice is (see you still see the 1" nori space after rolling).

10. Don't move the sushi mat yet and gently shape and tighten the roll with your fingers from outside of the mat. Shape the sushi roll into square shape (or round one). Then finally lift the sushi mat and rotate the roll once to seal the edge of nori. Again gently squeeze and tighten the roll with your fingers.

11. To cut a sushi roll, wet your knife with a damp towel and cut the roll in half first. You should "push then pull" the knife while cutting through the sushi. Wet the knife again and cut each half roll into 3 pieces. Serve with soy sauce, wasabi, and pickled ginger.

TO STORE

1. Sushi rolls should be consumed right away, but they can be stored in the refrigerator for up to 24 hours. I highly recommend keeping them in an airtight container or a plate wrapped tightly with plastic and then wrap around the container/plate with a thick kitchen towel so the food stay safe in a cool environment but rice doesn't get hard from cold air in the refrigerator.

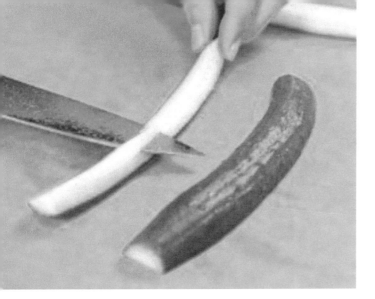 

Futomaki (Maki Sushi)

Learn how to make Futomaki, a traditional thick sushi roll typically filled with vegetables. You can easily prepare it ahead of time. It makes a great sushi roll to bring to festivals, potlucks or picnic.

 PREP TIME: 2 Hours   **COOK TIME:** 45 Minutes   Servings: 4 sushi rolls

Ingredients

4 sheets **nori (seaweed)**

pickled red ginger
(beni shoga or kizami beni shoga) (optional)

SUSHI RICE:
3 rice cooker cups
uncooked Japanese shortgrain rice

540 ml **water**

1 piece **kombu (dried kelp)** (2" x 2" or 5 cm x 5 cm; optional but it gives a nice aroma!)

SUSHI VINEGAR:
⅓ cup **rice vinegar** (80 ml)

3 Tbsp **sugar**

1½ tsp **kosher/sea salt**
(I use Diamond Crystal; Use half for table salt)

SEASONED SHIITAKE & KANPYO (GOURD

Instructions

SHIITAKE AND KANPYO

1. In a bowl (or a measuring cup), put 8 dried shiitake mushrooms and pour 1 cup water to cover the mushrooms. Place a smaller bowl on top so that mushrooms will stay submerged. Soak for 15 minutes.
2. In a small saucepan, bring water to a boil. Quickly rinse the kanpyo under running water and drain. Rub kanpyo with 1 tsp. salt. Rinse and drain well.
3. When the water is boiling, cook kanpyo for 3 minutes. Transfer to iced water to stop the cooking process and squeeze water out.
4. When the shiitake mushrooms are soft and tender, cut off and discard the stem. Strain the shiitake liquid through a fine sieve to remove any impurities.
5. If the reserved shiitake liquid is not 1 cup, add water until you have 1 cup.
6. In a medium saucepan, put the kanpyo and sliced mushrooms. Add 1 cup of reserved shiitake liquid into the saucepan.
7. Add 1 Tbsp. sugar, 1 Tbsp. mirin, and 1 Tbsp. soy sauce to the saucepan.
8. Bring it to a boil and once boiling, lower the heat to medium and cook until most of the liquid is gone, about 20-30 minutes.
9. Cut the shiitake mushrooms to very thin slices and squeeze the water out.
10. Squeeze the water out from kanpyo and cut into 8 inches (20 cm) length, which is about the same size as nori sheet.
11. When shiitake and kanpyo have cooled, keep in the fridge till the next day.

TAMAGOYAKI (DASHIMAKI TAMAGO)

1. Make 1 tamagoyaki or dashimaki tamago ahead of time and keep in the refrigerator to save time (see Recipe page 92).

STRIPS):
8 **dried shiitake mushrooms**

1 cup **water** (240 ml)

0.4 oz **dried kanpyo (gourd strips)** (10 g)

1 tsp **kosher/sea salt** (I use Diamond Crystal; Use half for table salt)

1 Tbsp **sugar**

1 Tbsp **mirin**

1 Tbsp **soy sauce**

OTHER FILLINGS:
tamagoyaki (recipe page 92)

a bunch mitsuba (Japanese parsley) (or spinach)

1 unagi (eel) (broiled)

1 Persian/Japanese cucumbers

1.4 oz **sakura denbu (seasoned cod fish flakes)** (40 g)

VINEGAR WATER FOR DIPPING HANDS (TEZU):
¼ cup **water** (60 ml)

2 tsp **rice vinegar**

2. Cut tamagoyaki into long strips store in the fridge till ready to use.

SUSHI RICE
First, make sushi rice. Sushi rice is steamed rice that is seasoned with rice vinegar, sugar, and salt. For 4 sushi rolls, you will need 3 rice cooker cups (1 cup = 180 ml) uncooked rice. (see Recipe page 200)

UNAGI (EEL)
The packaged unagi is already cooked. All you need to do is reheat in the oven. Set your oven to broil (high – 550°F/290°C) and preheat for 3 minutes. Line the baking sheet with aluminum foil. Spray a bit of oil on the aluminum foil and place the unagi on top. Put in the middle rack of your oven and broil for 5-7 minutes (no need to flip). Cut into 4 long strips.

MITSUBA OR SPINACH
1. Tie the stems with cooking twine. Bring a pot of water to a boil. Add 1 tsp. salt and blanch mitsuba or spinach just enough to tender. Do not overcook.
2. Soak the blanched mitsuba in iced water and squeeze the water out. Set aside.

CUCUMBER
Cut off the end and cut into quarter length wise and remove the seeds. Set aside.

SAKURA DENBU (SEASONED COD FISH FLAKES)
Open the package and put it in a small bowl. Set aside.

ASSEMBLE FUTOMAKI
1. Gather all the ingredients. Prepare *tezu* (vinegar water for dipping hands) by combining ¼ cup water and 2 tsp rice vinegar.
2. Place a bamboo sushi mat on the working surface or cutting board. Then place a sheet of nori on the bamboo mat, shiny side down. Divide sushi rice into quarters. Dip your fingers in *tezu*, and put ¼ of sushi rice on nori and spread evenly with your fingers. Make sure to wet your fingers with *tezu* when you do this. Spread the rice evenly; otherwise, your sushi roll won't look even when rolled.
3. Leaving about a ½ inch (1.5 cm) strip along the top of nori farthest away from you. Don't put the rice till the end because after you roll, the white rice could come out from the seam and it won't lookpretty.
4. Place the cucumber toward the bottom of nori. Front ingredients will need to go over the other ingredients. I recommend putting easy-to-hold ingredients toward the front, and put sakura denbu and shiita-

ke toward the top so the pieces won't fall down when you roll.

5. From the bottom end (of sushi rice), start rolling nori sheet over the filling tightly and firmly with bamboo mat until the bottom end reaches the end of sushi rice on top. Use your fingers to hold the ingredients when you roll.

6. Hold the top of the bamboo mat with one hand and hold the rolled bamboo mat with the other hand and pull against each other to tighten. Lift the bamboo mat and continue to roll. Place the bamboo mat over the roll and tightly squeeze. Continue to make the rest of the rolls.

7. Using a very sharp knife, cut the Futomaki in half first. Every slice or every other slice, wipe the knife with a wet kitchen cloth so that you can cut nicely.

8. Then cut each half into 3 pieces.

Temaki Sushi

Make sushi at home with simple hand rolled sushi called Temaki Sushi. Everyone in the family (or at the party) will have fun rolling the nori sheets around sushi rice and their favorite fillings!

 PREP TIME: 10 Minutes   Servings: 2 Temaki Sushi

Ingredients

½ cup sushi rice (cooked and seasoned)(90 g)

1 sheet **nori (seaweed)**

½ cup **fillings**

FOR FILLINGS:
sashimi grade fish of your choice (salmon, tuna, salmon roe, spicy tuna etc)

Persian/Japanese cucumbers

shiso leaves (Ooba) (perilla)

kaiware radish sprouts

takuan (pickled daikon radish)

avocado

carrot

toasted white sesame seeds

Instructions

1. If your raw fish comes as a block, slice the raw fish into long sticks. Or you can ask a fish monger at a Japanese grocery store to cut the raw fish for Temaki Sushi. They will cut fish into long sticks, instead of sashimi-style cut.
2. Cut nori in half.
3. Before you start, make sure your hands are dry in order to keep nori dry and crispy. Place the seaweed on the palm of your hand (shiny side down) and put a thin layer of rice on left third of nori.
4. Place fillings (shiso leaf, cucumber, raw fish and daikon radish sprouts) vertically across middle of middle of the rice.
5. Fold the bottom left corner of nori over and begin folding into cone shape.
6. Keep rolling until cone is formed. Put a piece of rice at the bottom right corner to use as glue and close tightly. Continue with the other half of the nori.
7. Serve with pickled ginger, wasabi, and soy sauce as condiments.

Temari Sushi

Celebrate happy occasions with these colorful ball-shaped Temari Sushi! Easily the prettiest sushi you can make at home or bring to a party or potluck!

 PREP TIME: 30 Minutes   **COOK TIME:** 30 Minutes   4 Servings (28 Temari Sushi)

Ingredients

5 rice cooker cups **sushi rice** (cooked and seasoned)

½ inch **lotus root (renkon)**

½ inch **carrot**

1 **large egg** (50 g w/o shell)

Pinch **kosher/sea salt** (I use Diamond Crystal; Use half for table salt)

2 slices **lemon**

¼ **avocado**

¼ cup **sakura denbu**

½ **sheet nori (seaweed)**

3 **shiso leaves** (Ooba) (Perilla)

1 Tbsp **neutral-flavored oil** (vegetable, rice bran, canola, etc)

SEASONING:
½ cup **dash**i (Japanese soup stock)

1 tsp **sake**

Instructions

1. Slice lotus root into thin silvers that resemble delicate flowers.
2. Thinly slice carrots and cut into flower-shape.
3. In a small saucepan, bring the seasoning to a boil and add lotus root and carrot. Cook until soft.
4. In a non-stick frying pan, heat oil over medium heat. In a bowl, whisk egg and salt together. Pour the egg mixture into the pan and spread evenly. Flip once the bottom side is cooked. When the egg is cooked, take it out and chiffonade the egg into thin strips.
5. Place a sheet of plastic wrap on top of the scale and measure 30g (2 Tbsp) of sushi rice and make a round ball. Transfer to a plate and measure the next batch. Make sure to cover the rice ball with plastic wrap and sushi rice with a damp towel to prevent the rice from drying.
6. Cut sashimi into thin slices.
7. Place a sheet of plastic wrap and lay down the sashimi of your choice. Put the sushi rice ball on top, wrap the plastic wrap around the rice. Twist and close the wrap tightly make a ball shape.
8. Continue with other ingredients.
9. Garnish with ikura, kaiware daikon, and other miniature greens.

1 tsp **mirin**

1 tsp **sugar**

2 tsp **usukuchi (lightcolor) soy sauce**
(or replace 2 tsp Usukuchi with 1 tsp
regular soy sauce + ¼ tsp salt)

Pinch **kosher/sea salt** (I use Diamond
Crystal; Use half for table salt)

YOUR SELECTION OF SASHIMI:
sashimi-grade salmon

sashimi-grade tuna (maguro)

sashimi-grade Sea Bream (tai)

sashimi-grade yellowtail (hamachi)

uni (sea urchin)

cooked shrimp

smoked salmon

Inari Sushi

Made of vinegared rice tucked inside little deep-fried tofu pockets, Inari Sushi is easily one of the easiest sushi to make at home. It's vegetarian and vegan friendly too!

 PREP TIME: 30 Minutes   Servings: 12 Inari Sushi

Ingredients

3-4 cups **sushi rice** (1 cup for approx 4 Inari Sushi)

1 Tbsp **toasted white sesame seeds**

12 **inari age (seasoned fried tofu pouch)**

the cooking liquid from inari age

12 **shiso leaves** (Optional)

12 **nori (seaweed)** (I used seasoned nori)

pickled red ginger (beni shoga or kizami beni shoga) (to garnish)

Instructions

1. Prepare sushi rice ahead of time and keep it at room temperature.
2. Add sesame seeds to the sushi rice and mix together.
3. Carefully open the inari age pocket (it's very thin, so it's easy to break). Make sure you can see the bottom of the pocket as you need to stuff the sushi rice all the way.
4. Moisten hands with the liquid from inari age. Take a small handful of rice and make a small rice ball. Do not make it too big, otherwise, it won't fit in inari age.
5. Wrap each rice ball with shiso if using and a piece of nori and stuff the rice ball into the inari age. Close the inari age and place open-end down on a plate.
6. Another method is to keep the bag open on top. Wrap each rice ball with a piece of nori and stuff the rice ball into the inari age. Then place shiso (if using) on top.
7. Tuck in the edge of inari age inside the pocket so you will have a nice smooth round edge. You can decorate the top as you like.
8. Serve with sushi ginger.

215

Chirashi Sushi

Chirashi Sushi is served on happy occasions and at parties in Japan. This bright and colorful dish is made of sushi rice with a variety of vegetables mixed in, and toppings sprinkled over the top.

 PREP TIME: 1 Hour   **COOK TIME:** 2 Hours   4 Servings

Ingredients

FOR PICKLED LOTUS ROOT & GINGER
2 inches **lotus root** (renkon) (5 cm)

1 knob **ginger** (1 inch, 2.5 cm)

½ cup **rice vinegar** (120 ml)

⅓ cup **sugar** (65 g)

½ tsp **kosher/sea salt** (I use Diamond Crystal; Use half for table salt)

FOR CHIRASHI SUSHI MIX
4 **dried shiitake mushrooms**

½ cup **water** (120 ml) (for soaking dried shiitake mushrooms)

⅔ **gobo** (burdock root)

0.8 oz **dried kanpyo (gourd strips)** (20 g)

Instructions

TO MAKE PICKLED LOTUS ROOT & GINGER:

1. Combine rice vinegar, sugar, and kosher salt in a small saucepan. Bring it to a boil and let the sugar dissolved completely. Set aside to cool.
2. Peel and cut the ginger to julienne strips (thinner the better). Peel the lotus root and cut out the edge to make a flower shape (hana renkon).
3. Slice the lotus root into ⅛" (3 mm) and soak in vinegar water for 5 minutes to prevent from turning brown (just drop a few rice vinegar in water).
4. Boil water in a small saucepan and blanch the ginger and lotus root for 3 minutes. Drain well and transfer them to the vinegar mixture to marinate. You can make this ahead and keep it up to 1 week in refrigerator.

TO MAKE CHIRASHI SUSHI MIX:

1. Soak dried shiitake mushrooms with ½ cup water until they are hydrated and tender. Then squeeze the mushrooms and reserve the liquid (= shiitake dashi) in the bowl. Cut off and discard the stem.
2. Slice the shiitake mushrooms. Strain the reserved shiitake dashi to remove impurities. Save this shiitake dashi until you're ready to use.
3. Make a criss-cross incision at one end of the gobo. This will help you shave the gobo like a pencil. Shave into small thin pieces as you rotate the gobo. Soak the cut pieces in water so they won't turn brown. Change the water 1-2 times. Drain right before you start cooking.
4. In a small saucepan, bring water to a boil. Quickly rinse the kanpyo in running water and drain. Rub kanpyo with 1 tsp salt. Rinse and drain well.
5. When the water is boiling cook kanpyo for 3 minutes. Transfer to iced water to stop cooking process and squeeze water out.

1 tsp **kosher/sea salt** (I use Diamond Crystal; Use half for table salt) (for rubbing kanpyo)

½ **carrot**

1 ¼ cup **dashi** (Japanese soup stock) (300 ml)

¼ cup **sake** (60 m)

3 Tbsp **mirin**

1 Tbsp **sugar**

2 Tbsp **soy sauce**

FOR EGG CREPE (KINSHI TAMAGO)
3 **large eggs** (50 g each w/o shell)

1 Tbsp **sugar** (optional)

1 Tbsp **dashi** (Japanese soup stock) (or sake or water)

¼ tsp **kosher/sea salt** (I use Diamond Crystal; Use half for table salt)

½ Tbsp **neutral-flavored oil** (vegetable, canola, etc)

FOR SNOW PEAS
6 **snow peas**

pinch **kosher/sea salt** (I use Diamond Crystal;

6. Cut kanpyo into small pieces and cut the carrot into julienne strips.
7. Add shiitake mushrooms, gobo, and kanpyo in the pot (keep the carrot aside for now). Add dashi, reserved shiitake dashi (the liquid from hydrating dried shiitake), sake, mirin, sugar, and soy sauce, and bring to a simmer on medium heat.
8. Skim the foam and scum on the surface as much as you can, decrease the heat to simmer, and cover with otoshibuta (drop lid). This lid ensures that ingredients are submerged under the liquid and flavorful cooking liquid circulates well. You can make one with aluminum foil easily.
9. Add the carrot toward the end while there is still liquid in the pot so it doesn't get overcooked. Continue to cook with Otoshibuta until the liquid is almost gone. The whole cooking process is about 20-25 minutes depending on the heat. Transfer the Chirashi Sushi Mix to a plate to cool completely. If you end up with some cooking liquid, you can save some so you can season the rice later. You can make this ahead and keep it in the refrigerator up to 3-4 days.

TO MAKE EGG CREPES:
1. Whisk the eggs and add the rest of the ingredients into the bowl. Whisk to combine and strain the egg mixture to get a silky texture.
2. Heat the large non-stick frying pan and grease the pan with a paper towel dipped in vegetable oil. Make sure to wipe off the excess oil. When the pan is hot, pour the egg mixture just enough to cover the bottom of the entire fry pan.
3. Tilt to fill the frying pan with the egg mixture and cover with the lid. Remove from the heat and place the pan on a cold towel to cool so the egg won't become brown. Once the egg crepe is cooked through, transfer to a wire rack and let cool completely. Continue this process until all the egg mixture is gone.
4. Roll up the egg crepes and cut thinly into julienned strips. Loosen them up and set aside. You can make this ahead and keep it in the refrigerator up to 2-3 days or freeze up to 4 weeks.

TO PREPARE SNOW PEAS:
Remove the tough strings along the edges of snow peas. Bring water to a boil in a small saucepan. Add a pinch of salt and blanch them for 2 minutes. Drain and cut diagonally in half or thirds.

TO MAKE SUSHI RICE:
Rinse the rice, soak for 30 minutes, and drain. Put the rice in a rice cooker bowl and add the water till "Sushi" water level (a bit less than regular). Place kombu on top and start cooking. Combine the sushi vinegar ingredients in a bowl and mix together. You can microwave

Use half for table salt)

FOR SUSHI RICE
3 rice cooker cups
uncooked Japanese shortgrain rice (540 ml)

540 ml **water**

2 inch **kombu (dried kelp)** (5 cm)

⅓ cup **rice vinegar** (80 ml)

3 Tbsp **sugar**

1 ½ tsp **kosher/sea salt** (I use Diamond Crystal; Use half for table salt)

FOR UNAGI (EELS)
1 package **unagi (eel)** (160 g)

FOR SHRIMP
8-10 **large shrimp**

1 Tbsp **sake**

pinch **kosher/sea salt** (I use Diamond Crystal; Use half for table salt)

TOPPINGS (OPTIONAL)
4 Tbsp **ikura (salmon roe)**

4 Tbsp **shredded nori seaweed (kizami nori)**

½ Tbsp **toasted white sesame seeds**

or heat the mixture in a saucepan over the stove to dissolve the sugar completely.

TO PREPARE UNAGI
The packaged unagi is already cooked. All you need to do is reheat in the oven. Set your oven to broil (high – 550°F/290°C) and preheat for 3 minutes. Line the baking sheet with aluminum foil. Spray a bit of oil on the aluminum foil and place the unagi on top. Put in the middle rack of your oven and broil for 5-7 minutes (no need to flip). Once it's cool to touch, you can cut into ¼ inch (0.6 mm) pieces. Set aside.

TO PREPARE SHRIMP:
Using a skewer, devein shrimp without removing shell (page 280). Peel the shell after cooking to retain the flavor of the shrimp. Boil water in a medium saucepan. Once boiling, add sake and shrimp and simmer until pink, about 2-3 minutes. Remove the shell and set aside.

TO ASSEMBLE CHIRASHI SUSHI:
1. Start this step when all the above steps are completed. Discard the kombu from sushi rice and transfer to *sushi oke/hangiri* (or a large serving platter). If you use sushi oke, quickly run water so rice doesn't stick. Pour sushi vinegar over the rice paddle to distribute evenly over the rice. With the rice paddle, slice at a 45 degree angle to separate the rice instead of mixing. At the same time use a fan to cool the rice so it will shine and doesn't get mushy.
2. Once the sushi rice is cooled, squeeze the Chirashi Sushi Mix to remove excess liquid (otherwise rice gets too soggy) and combine with sushi rice. You can always add a few Tbsp of reserved liquid to season the rice if you like (I don't usually do it).
3. Gather all the toppings you've prepared.
4. First, spread the shredded egg crepe. Decorate the chirashi sushi as you like. I usually start from lotus root, shrimp, unagi, snow peas, ikura, sesame seeds, and nori in the center. Enjoy!

Dragon Roll

Learn how to make your all-time favorite Dragon Roll at home! In this recipe, we will talk about the key ingredients and tips & tricks to make the perfect sushi roll.

 PREP TIME: 1 Hour   Servings: 4 Dragon Rolls

Ingredients

1 **Persian/Japanese cucumbers**

2 **avocados**

½ **lemon** (optional)

2 sheets **nori (seaweed)** (cut in half crosswise)

2 cups sushi rice (360 g cooked and seasoned) (each roll needs ½ cup sushi rice)(Recipe page 200)

8 pieces **shrimp tempura**

2 Tbsp **tobiko (flying fish roe)** (20g)

unagi (eel) (optional)

spicy mayo

unagi sauce (page 270)

toasted black sesame seeds

Instructions

1. Cut cucumber lengthwise into quarters. Remove the seeds and then cut in half lengthwise.
2. Cut the avocado in half lengthwise around the seed and twist the two halves until they separate. Hack the knife edge into the pit. Hold the skin of the avocado with the other hand and twist in counter directions. The pit will come out smoothly.
3. Remove the skin and slice the avocado widthwise.
4. Gently press the avocado slices with your fingers and then keep pressing gently and evenly with the side of the knife until the length of avocado is about the length of sushi roll (length of nori seaweed). If you don't serve the sushi roll right away, I recommend squeezing lemon over the avocado to prevent discoloration.
5. Wrap the bamboo mat with plastic wrap and place half of the nori sheet, shiny side down. Dip your hands in tezu (vinegar water) and spread ½ cup sushi rice over the nori sheet.
6. Turn it over and put the shrimp tempura, cucumber strips, and tobiko at the bottom end of the nori sheet. If you like to put unagi, place inside here as well.
7. From the bottom end, start rolling nori sheet over the filling tightly and firmly with bamboo mat until the bottom end reaches the nori sheet. Lift the bamboo mat and roll over.
8. Place the bamboo mat over the roll and give it a tight squeeze.
9. Using the side of the knife, place the avocado on top of the roll.
10. Place plastic wrap over the roll and then put the bamboo mat over. Tightly squeeze the roll until the avocado slices wrap around the sushi. Be gentle so you won't break the avocado slices.
11. Cut the roll into 8 pieces with the knife. Clean knife with a wet towel after each cut. If the roll gets messy, tightly squeeze the sushi roll again with the bamboo mat. Remove the plastic wrap on top of the sushi and transfer it to a serving plate.

VINEGAR WATER (TEZU)

¼ cup **water**

2 tsp **rice vinegar**

12. Put tobiko on each piece of sushi and drizzle spicy mayo and sprinkle black sesame seeds on top. If you like, place some unagi sauce on the plate so you can dip the sushi. Enjoy!

JAPANESE PARTY DISHES

Sukiyaki

Cozy up at your get-together with friends and family with this homemade sukiyaki recipe. This hot pot is served with seared marbled beef and a variety of vegetables cooked in a soy sauce broth.

 PREP TIME: 20 Minutes   **COOK TIME:** 10 Minutes   4 Servings

Ingredients

SUKIYAKI INGREDIENTS
2 servings **udon noodles** (Typically added to the soup at the end of the meal)

½ head **napa cabbage** (about 10 leaves or 1.5 lbs or 690 g)

½ bunch **shungiku** (Tong Ho/Garland Chrysanthemum) (7 oz or 200 g)

1 **negi** (long green onion) (leek or 3 green onions)

1 package **enoki mushrooms**

8 **shiitake mushrooms** (carve decorative shapes)

1 package **yaki tofu** (Broiled Tofu) (9 oz or 255 g)

Instructions

TO MAKE SUKIYAKI SAUCE

Combine 1 cup sake, 1 cup mirin, ¼ cup sugar, and 1 cup soy sauce in a small saucepan and bring it to a boil. Once boiling, turn off the heat and set aside. This Sukiyaki sauce can be stored in an air-tight container in the refrigerator for up to a month.

TO PREPARE THE INGREDIENTS

1. If your udon is frozen, cook it in boiling water until loosen. Otherwise, follow the udon package instructions. Remove from heat and soak in iced water to prevent overcooking. Drain and transfer to a plate covered with plastic. You will not need it till the end of the sukiyaki meal.
2. Prepare sukiyaki ingredients. Cut napa cabbage into 2" (5 cm) wide then cut in half right at the middle of the white part.
3. Cut shungiku into 2" (5 cm) wide, and slice Tokyo negi. Discard the bottom part of enoki mushroom and tear into smaller bundles.
4. Discard the shiitake stem and decorate the top of shiitake if you like.
5. Cut tofu into smaller pieces (I usually cut into 6-8 pieces).
6. If you like, you can slice some carrots and then stamp them into a floral shape for decoration.
7. Drain and rinse the shirataki noodles. Put all the ingredients on one big platter for the table or into smaller individual servings.

TO COOK SUKIYAKI

1. Set a portable gas cooktop at the dining table. Each person should have a medium-sized bowl where the cooked food is being transfered to from the pot. Heat a cast iron sukiyaki pot (or any pot) on medium heat. When it's hot, add 1 Tbsp cooking oil (or beef fat).
2. Place 2-4 slices of well-marbled beef to sear and sprinkle 1 Tbsp brown sugar. Flip and cook the other side of the meat. You can pour a little bit of Sukiyaki Sauce over the meat and enjoy some of the

⅓ **carrot** (for decoration, optional)

1 package **shirataki noodles** (7 oz or 198 g)

1 lb **thinly sliced beef** (chuck or rib eye) (454 g)

TO COOK SUKIYAKI
1 Tbsp **neutral-flavored oil (vegetable, rice bran, canola, etc)**

1 Tbsp **brown sugar**

1 ½ cup **dashi** (360 ml)

SUKIYAKI SAUCE
(YIELD 2 ⅔ CUP)
1 cup **sake** (240 ml)

1 cup **mirin** (240 ml)

¼ cup **sugar** (60 ml)

1 cup **soy sauce** (240 ml)

sweet and nicely caramelized meat (this is to enjoy the good quality meat), and continue to the next step.

THE FIRST ROUND OF SUKIYAKI

1. Pour half of the Sukiyaki Sauce you made (1 ⅓ cup) and 1 cup dashi (or water) in the pot.
2. Add vegetables, tofu, and other ingredients to the pot (keep the udon for later). Add more Sukiyaki Sauce or dashi (or water) if necessary. The ⅔ of the ingredients should be submerged in the broth. Put the lid on and bring to a gentle boil. Once boiling, turn down the heat and simmer until the ingredients are cooked through. Once ingredients are cooked through, you can add more beef as the meat will cook fast. Enjoy the first round of sukiyaki. *Tip: If the sauce gets too salty add dashi (or water) to dilute. If the vegetables diluted the sauce too much, then add more sauce.*

THE SECOND/THIRD ROUND OF SUKIYAKI (OPTIONAL)

When there is less cooked food in the pot, divide the leftover into individual bowls. Then start cooking the second round by adding more ingredients to the pot (repeat the previous step). While the second round of sukiyaki is being cooked, you can enjoy the leftovers from the first pot or any side dishes.

TO END THE MEAL

We usually end the sukiyaki meal with udon. When most of the ingredients have disappeared, add udon to the pot. Cook until heated through and enjoy.

Shabu Shabu

Shabu Shabu is a popular Japanese-style hot pot where the meat and assorted vegetables are cooked in a flavorful broth called kombu dashi. Everyone at the table takes part in the cooking and enjoys the ingredients with different dipping sauces. It's intimate yet casual, and a whole lot of fun!

 PREP TIME: 15 Minutes   **COOK TIME:** 15 Minutes   4 Servings

Ingredients

1 **kombu** (dried kelp) (10 g, 3" x 3" or 7.5 cm x 7.5 cm)

1 package **udon noodles** (9 oz/250 g) (I like Sanuki Udon)

8 leaves **napa cabbage** (12 oz/340 g)

½ bunch **shungiku** (Tong Ho/Garland Chrysanthemum) (4 oz/113 g)

1 **negi** (long green onion) (4 oz/113 g)(Use 2 green onions)

1 **package enoki mushrooms** (7 oz/200 g)

1 package **shimeji mushrooms** (3.5 oz/100 g)

4 **shiitake mushrooms**

Instructions

TO PREPARE BROTH

Fill a donabe (Dutch oven or any large pot) two-thirds full with water. Add kombu and soak in water for at least 30 minutes.

TO PREPARE INGREDIENTS

1. Prepare udon noodles according to the instructions. If you use frozen udon, simply add in boiling water and reheat for 1 minute. Transfer to iced water to stop cooking and drain well. Serve on a plate and set aside.
2. Cut napa cabbages into 2-inch (5 cm) pieces, and then cut each piece into half or thirds.
3. Cut the shungiku into 2-inch (5 cm) pieces.
4. We only use the white part of negi (green onion/leeks). Cut it diagonally into ½ inch (1.3 cm) thick pieces.
5. Rinse enoki and shimeji mushrooms. Discard the bottom of both mushrooms and separate into smaller chunks.
6. Cut the stem of shiitake mushrooms. If you like, you can do a decorative cutting.
7. Cut the carrot into ¼ inch rounds. If you like, you can use a vegetable cutter to create a flower shape.
8. Cut the tofu into 1 inch (2.5 cm) thick square pieces.
9. Arrange all the ingredients on a serving platter.
10. Peel daikon and grate using a grater. Squeeze grated daikon gently and put in a small bowl.
11. Cut the green onions into thin rounds and put it in a bowl.
12. Prepare shichimi togarashi in a bowl (optional). Lay the thinly sliced beef on a plate.

TO COOK SHABU SHABU

(2.3 oz/65 g)

2 inches **carrot** (2.3 oz/65 g)

1 package **medium-firm tofu** (14 oz/396 g)

1 lb **thinly sliced beef** (chuck or rib eye) (450 g) (4-5 oz/113-140 g per person)

TO SERVE
2 inches **daikon radish** (5 oz/143 g)

2 **green onions/ scallions** (0.9 oz/25 g)

shichimi togarashi (Japanese seven spice)

sesame sauce

ponzu

1. Set a portable gas burner and put the donabe on the stove. Place platters with ingredients on the table. Give each person a ponzu sauce and sesame sauce. I also like to prepare an additional bowl for each person so they can use it to cool the food.
2. Bring the broth to a simmer over medium heat. Take out the kombu right before water starts to boil (otherwise, the water gets slimy).
3. Add the tofu, the tough part of napa cabbage and shungiku, negi, carrots, and some mushrooms. Cook the ingredients in batches. Cover to cook for 10 minutes.

TO EAT SHABU SHABU
1. While you're waiting for the food to cook, prepare your dipping sauces. Add grated daikon, shichimi togarashi, and green onion in ponzu, and green onion in sesame sauce.
2. When you want to eat meat, pick up a slice of thinly sliced beef with a set of communal chopsticks and stir the meat in the boiling broth to cook for 20-30 seconds, or until no longer pink. Do not overcook.
3. Take out the cooked beef and vegetables from the pot when they are done, and dip the food in ponzu or sesame sauce.
4. Add remaining ingredients in the boiling broth as needed and simmer for a few minutes. Skim off the scum and fat from the broth as you repeat cooking. Prepare a fine mesh skimmer and a 2-cup measuring cup or bowl filled with water at the table so you can skim as you cook. Water in the measuring cup will help you get rid of scum from the skimmer.
5. When all the ingredients are cooked, skim the broth for udon noodles. Typically, hot pot meal ends with cooking udon noodles or porridge.
6. Add udon noodles in the pot and reheat for 1-2 minutes. Lightly season the udon soup with salt and white pepper, if you like.
7. Dilute the ponzu sauce with the broth and serve udon noodles.

Oden (Japanese Fish Cake Stew)

A classic winter comfort dish in Japan, Oden is a one-pot dish with an assortment of fish balls, fish cakes, deep-fried tofu, hard-boiled eggs, konnyaku and some vegetables simmered in soy sauce-based dashi broth.

 PREP TIME: 1 Hour   **COOK TIME:** 3 Hours   6 Servings

Ingredients

ODEN BROTH:
8 cups **dashi** (Japanese soup stock) (1920 ml)

4 Tbsp **usukuchi (lightcolor) soy sauce** (It's not a low-sodium soy sauce) (60 ml)

2 Tbsp **soy Sauce**

2 Tbsp **sake**

1 Tbsp **sugar**

1 Tbsp **mirin**

¼ tsp **kosher/sea salt** (I use Diamond Crystal; Use half for table salt) (to taste)

ODEN INGREDIENTS:
8 inch **daikon radish** (20 cm)

5 **large eggs** (50 g each w/o shell)

5 strips **nishime kombu** (dried seaweed)

4 oz **octopus sashimi** (13 g)

Instructions

1. In a donabe (earthenware pot), make dashi (Japanese soup stock) and add Seasonings.
2. Slice daikon into 1-inch pieces and remove the skin (you can peel first before cutting).
3. Remove the corners (mentori technique) so there are no sharp edges. This will prevent daikon from breaking into pieces.
4. If you prepare rice to serve with Oden, preserve the white water from cleaning rice. Put daikon and the white water in a small pot and start cooking until a skewer goes through (do not cover the lid). In Japan, we say the rice water will get rid of bitterness and the smell from daikon. The water also gives daikon a nice white color. Make sure to cook daikon from cold water so the center gets cooked slowly before boiling and that will help cook daikon evenly.
5. Boil eggs (cook from cold water, after boiling set timer for 12 minutes, run cold water and peel off shells).
6. Cut nishime kombu into short pieces and quickly rinse the coating in running water. Make a knot like below.
7. Cut and skewer the octopus.
8. Cut konnyaku into smaller pieces. Typically triangle shape.
9. Add the konnyaku in water and bring it to a boil. After boiling, cook for 1 minute and drain. Set aside.
10. Put water in a big pot and bring water to a boil in a large pot. Add nerimono (Japanese fish cakes and fish balls) in boiling water to get rid of excess oil – just for 15-30 seconds. Drain and set aside. Cut big pieces into halves. Do the second batch if Nerimono didn't fit in a pot.

1 pkg konnyaku (konjac)(9 oz, 255 g)

1 **negi** (long green onion) (chopped, optional)

2 packages **oden set** (Japanese fish cakes and fish balls)

1 **aburaage** (deep-fried tofu pouch) (for mochi packets)

1 **kirimochi or homemade mochi** (for mochi packets)

1 inch **carrot** (cut into Flower Petals, optional)

Japanese karashi hot mustard (optional; to serve)

11. Make mochi-filled tofu bags. Quickly run aburaage (fried bean curd) in boiling water to remove excess oil. Drain and cut in half. Cut mochi into half. Open one side of aburaage so you can put mochi in it. Use a toothpick or kombu to tie the aburaage so the mochi won't fall out.
12. Put everything except for nerimono and mochi bag in the donabe and cook covered over low heat for 2-3 hours minimum. Skim off the scum and fat along the way.
13. Add nerimono and mochi bag and cook for 30 minutes (or longer) over low heat.
14. Cover and reheat when you are ready to serve. I usually let them soak for overnight (after cool down, keep in the fridge) and eat the next day. Oden is often served with Karashi (hot mustard).

Okonomiyaki

Hailing from Osaka, Okonomiyaki is a delicious Japanese savory pancake made with flour, eggs, cabbage, and protein, and topped with a variety of condiments.

 PREP TIME: 30 Minutes   **COOK TIME:** 30 Minutes   4 Servings

Ingredients

1 cup **all-purpose flour** (plain flour) (120 g)

¼ tsp **kosher/sea salt** (I use Diamond Crystal; Use half for table salt)

¼ tsp **sugar**

¼ tsp **baking powder**

2-3 inch **nagaimo/yamaimo** (5-8 cm, 160 g, 5.6 oz)

¾ cup **dashi (Japanese soup stock)** (180 ml; You can make Dashi or use ¾ cup water + 1 tsp dashi powder. For vegetarian, use Kombu Dashi.)

1 **large cabbage head** (1.6 lb or 740 g)

½ lb **sliced pork belly** (227 g; You can thinly slice the pork belly if your pork belly is a slab. You can sub with shrimp or squid. For vegetarian, skip and use

Instructions

TO PREPARE OKONOMIYAKI BATTER

1. In a large bowl, combine 1 cup (120 g) all-purpose flour, ¼ tsp salt, ¼ tsp sugar, and ¼ tsp baking powder and mix all together.
2. Peel and grate nagaimo in a small bowl. It can get itchy, so work quickly and rinse your hand right after. Nagaimo is very slimy and slippery, so make sure you have a good grip.
3. Add the grated nagaimo and dashi in the bowl.
4. Mix all together till combined. Cover the bowl with and let it rest in the refrigerator for at least one hour.

TO MAKE OKONOMIYAKI SAUCE

1. Meanwhile, gather all the ingredients for Okonomiyaki Sauce.
2. Combine 1 ½ Tbsp sugar, 2 Tbsp oyster sauce, 4 Tbsp ketchup, and 3 ½ Tbsp Worcestershire sauce in a small bowl. Mix all together until sugar is completely dissolved.

TO PREPARE OKONOMIYAKI

1. Discard the core of the cabbage and then mince the cabbage leaves.
2. Cut the pork belly slices in half and set aside.
3. Take out the batter from the refrigerator and add 4 large eggs, ½ cup (8 Tbsp) tempura scraps (tenkasu/agedama), and ¼ cup (4 Tbsp) pickled red ginger (Kizami Beni Shoga) in the bowl. Mix until well-combined.
4. Add chopped cabbage to the batter ⅓ at a time. Mix well before adding the rest.

TO GRILL OKONOMIYAKI

1. In a large pan, heat vegetable oil on medium heat. When the

mushroom.)

4 **large eggs** (50 g each w/o shell)

½ cup **tenkasu/agedama** (tempura scraps) (8 Tbsp)

¼ cup **pickled red ginger** (beni shoga or kizami beni shoga) (4 Tbsp)

neutral-flavored oil (vegetable, canola, etc)

OKONOMIYAKI SAUCE
1 ½ Tbsp **sugar**

2 Tbsp **oyster sauce**

4 Tbsp **ketchup**

3 ½ Tbsp **Worcestershire sauce**

TOPPINGS
okonomi sauce

Japanese mayonnaise

katsuobushi (dried bonito flakes) (Skip for vegetarian)

aonori (dried green seaweed)

green onions/scallions

pickled red ginger (beni shoga or kizami beni shoga)

frying pan is hot (400°F or 200°C), spread the batter in a circle on the pan. We like thicker okonomiyaki (final thickness is ¾ inches or 2cm). If you're new to making okonomiyaki, make a smaller and thinner size so it's easier to flip.
2. Place 2-3 sliced pork belly on top of okonomiyaki and cook covered for 5 minutes.
3. When the bottom side is nicely browned, flip over.
4. Gently press the okonomiyaki to fix the shape and keep it together. Cover and cook for another 5 minutes.
5. Flip over one last time and cook uncovered for 2 minutes. If you're going to cook the next batch, transfer to a plate.

TO SERVE

Here are the ingredients for toppings. Apply okonomiyaki sauce with brush, add Japanese mayonnaise in zigzagging lines (optional), and sprinkle dried bonito flakes (katsuobushi). You can also put dried green seaweed (aonori), chopped green onions, and pickled red ginger on top for garnish.

TO STORE

Okonomiyaki freezes well. Once it cools down (no sauce or toppings), wrap each okonomiyaki in aluminum foil and put it in a freezer bag. When you want to eat it, defrost first and put it in a toaster oven or oven to heat it up. It's a great quick meal!

TO COOK SEVERAL OKONOMIYAKI AT ONCE

If you have a Japanese griddle with a lid (We call it "Hot Plate"), you can cook several okonomiyaki at once! Otherwise, I recommend cooking two okonomiyaki (each in one frying pan) at a time.

Takoyaki

Takoyaki, or Octopus Balls, are one of Japan's best-known street food originated in Osaka. Whether you make the traditional style with bits of octopus or other alternatives, these ball-shape dumplings are fun to make with your friends and family!

 PREP TIME: 15 Minutes   **COOK TIME:** 10 Minutes   Servings: 26 Pieces

Ingredients

FOR COOKING TAKOYAKI
¼ cup **katsuobushi** (dried bonito flakes) (3 g)

2 **green onions/scallions**

1 Tbsp **pickled red ginger** (beni shoga or kizami beni shoga)

4.2 oz **cooked octopus** (120 g; Cooked octopus can be purchased in Japanese grocery stores. Not a fan of octopus? You can include veggies (my kids love corn), cheese, small mochi pieces... choices are endless!)

2 Tbsp **neutral-flavored oil** (vegetable, canola, etc)

⅓ cup **tenkasu/agedama** (tempura scraps) (15 g)

TAKOYAKI BATTER
1 cup **all-purpose flour** (plain flour) (4.2 oz, 120 g)

2 tsp **baking powder**

½ tsp **kosher/sea salt** (I use

Instructions

TO PREPARE FILLINGS

1. Grind ¼ cup (4g) katsuobushi (bonito flakes) into fine powder. Set aside, we'll use this powder when we're cooking Takoyaki.
2. Cut green onions into fine slices and mince 1 Tbsp red pickled ginger.
3. Cut octopus into ½ inch (1.3 cm) bite-size pieces. I use "rangiri" cutting technique.

TO MAKE TAKOYAKI BATTER

1. In a large mixing bowl, combine 1 cup (4.2 oz/120 g) all-purpose flour, 2 tsp baking powder, and ½ tsp kosher salt and whisk all together.
2. Add 2 large eggs, 1 tsp soy sauce, and 1 ½ cup (360 ml) dashi.
3. Whisk all together until well-blended and transfer the batter to a 2-cup measuring cup with a handle (or any other pitcher with a spout for easy pouring).

TO COOK TAKOYAKI

1. Heat the takoyaki pan to 400°F (200°C) over medium heat. Using a brush, generously oil the takoyaki pan (both the holes and connecting flat areas). When the pan starts smoking, pour the batter to fill the holes. It's okay for the batter to slightly overflow the holes.
2. Add 1-3 octopus pieces in each hole depending on its size and sprinkle katsuobushi powder on top.
3. Then sprinkle tenkasu, green onion, and pickled red ginger.

Diamond Crystal; Use half for table salt)

2 **large eggs** (50 g each w/o shell)

1 tsp **soy sauce**

1 ½ cup **dashi** (Japanese soup stock) (360 ml)

TOPPING
½ cup **takoyaki sauce** (or use Tonkatsu sauce; drizzle as much as you need)(120 ml)

Japanese mayonnaise (drizzle as much as you need)

katsuobushi (dried bonito flakes) (sprinkle on top)

Aonori (dried green seaweed) (sprinkle on top)

4. After 3 minutes or so, when the bottom of the balls has hardened slightly, break the connected batter between each ball with skewers. Then turn each piece a 90° degree, stuffng in the edges as you are turning. The batter will flow out from the inside of each takoyaki ball and creates the other side of the takoyaki ball. After you finish flipping, set timer for 4 minutes. Keep turning constantly so each piece will have nice round shape.

5. Home takoyaki grill doesn't equally distribute heat so it's a good idea to swap takoyaki balls around to achieve an even color. Transfer takoyaki balls onto a plate and drizzle with the sauce and mayonnaise. Finish off by light sprinkles of katsuobushi and dried green seaweed. Serve immediately (the inside is VERY hot - be careful!).

Yakiniku Sauce

Yakiniku sauce is a sweet & flavorful Japanese BBQ sauce. It's perfect for dipping thin slices of well-marbled short ribs and other grilled goodies.

PREP TIME: 5 Minutes

COOK TIME: 5 Minutes

STEEPING TIME: 8 Hours

3 Servings (⅓ cup, 100 ml)

Ingredients

FOR THE SAUCE
2 Tbsp **sake**

2 Tbsp **mirin**

1 tsp **sugar**

½ tsp **rice vinegar**

3 Tbsp **soy sauce**

½ tsp **miso**

¼ tsp **katsuobushi (dried bonito flakes)**

⅛ **apple** (I used a fuji apple)

2 tsp **toasted white sesame seeds**

Instructions

MAKE THE SAUCE A DAY BEFORE
1. Gather all the ingredients. I highly recommend making the sauce a day before.
2. In a small saucepan, add sake, mirin, sugar, rice vinegar, soy sauce, miso, katsuobushi, and simmer for 1 ½ minute.
3. Strain the sauce. If you plan to preserve the sauce for a longer time, pour it into a mason jar (or airtight container). Do not add grated apple and sesame seeds yet. It will last longer without the grated apple. Keep refrigerated for up to a month.
4. Add the sesame seeds and grated apple to the sauce. Now it's ready to use. Let the sauce sit overnight in the refrigerator to meld all the flavors together.

TO STORE
5. Store in the refrigerator and use it within 3 days.

Yakitori

Glazed in a savory sweet sauce, these chicken and scallion skewers (Negima) are hard to resist! You'd love this simple yakitori recipe. It's great for grilling outdoor or under the broiler!

 PREP TIME: 30 Minutes   **COOK TIME:** 12 Minutes   Servings: 10 Yakitori Skewers

Ingredients

1 lb **boneless, skinless chicken thighs** (454 g; at room temperature)

9 **green onions/scallions**

neutral-flavored oil (vegetable, canola, etc)

YAKITORI SAUCE (TARE):
½ cup **soy sauce** (120 ml)

½ cup **mirin** (120 ml)

¼ cup **sake** (60 ml)

¼ cup **water** (60 ml)

2 tsp **brown sugar** (packed tsp)

Instructions

Soak about 10 to 12 (5-inch) bamboo skewers in water for 30 minutes.

TO MAKE YAKITORI SAUCE (TARE)

1. In a small saucepan, add mirin, soy sauce, sake, water, brown sugar, and the green part of 1 scallion, and bring it to a boil over high heat. Once boiling, reduce the heat to low and simmer, uncovered, until the liquid is reduced by half. It will take about 30 minutes. The sauce will thicken with a glossy shine. Let it cool to room temperature before using.
2. Reserve ⅓ of the sauce in a small bowl for final coating (Use this sauce after the chicken is cooked). Note: You can make the sauce ahead of time. Put only the sauce (no green onion) in a mason jar. Store in the refrigerator for up to 2-3 months in the refrigerator.

TO PREPARE YAKITORI

1. Cut the white and light green part of scallions into 1 inch pieces.
2. Cut chicken into 1-inch cubes.
3. On a flat work surface, fold each slice of chicken in half, insert into the chicken at 45 degrees angle, and press down on the skewer to pierce through the center.
4. 4. Alternate each chicken slice with a piece of scallion lined up perpendicular to the skewer. Each skewer will hold about 4 chicken slices and 3 scallion pieces.

TO GRILL (BROIL) YAKITORI

1. Grease the grate of the broiler/wire rack (or oven-safe cooling rack) to avoid the chicken sticking on the grate. Place the skewers on top.
2. Set the broiler to high and wait until the heating elements are hot. Broil for 6 minutes.
3. Take out 2 Tbsp of the Yakitori Sauce in a small bowl for brushing (you do not want to cross contaminate). After 6 minutes, brush the sauce on

the meat on both sides and continue to broil for 3-4 minutes to caramel-ize the sauce.

4. Transfer the skewers to a serving plate. Using a clean brush, brush the chicken on top with the reserved sauce. *Tip: If you accidentally cross-contaminate, you have to boil the sauce again.* Serve and enjoy!

DESSERTS

Mitarashi Dango

Mitarashi Dango is a traditional Japanese rice dumpling smothered in an irresistibly sweet soy glaze. The dumplings are skewered on a bamboo stick and enjoyed all year round. Make this street snack right in your own kitchen!

 PREP TIME: 30 Minutes   **COOK TIME:** 15 Minutes   Servings: 5 Skewers (16-17 balls)

Ingredients

IF YOU'RE USING JOSHINKO & SHIRATAMAKO
⅔ cup **joshinko (Japanese rice flour)** (100 g)

¾ cup **shiratamako (glutinous rice flour/ sweet rice flour)** (100 g)

⅔ cup **warm water** (roughly ⅔ cup; joshinko requires warm water)(150-160 ml)

IF YOU'RE USING DANGOKO
7 oz **dangoko (Japanese rice dumpling flour)** (200 g)

⅔ cup **water** (roughly 140-150 ml)

SWEET SOY GLAZE:

Instructions

1. Whether you decide to use joshinko & shiratamako OR dangoko, the method is the same.
2. Gather ingredients for the sweet soy glaze. Soak the skewers in water. You can start boiling a large pot of water on low heat.

TO MAKE DANGO (RICE DUMPLINGS)

1. Combine shiratamako and joshinko in a bowl (or add just Dangoko in a bowl).
2. Stir in warm water (or cold water for Dangoko) a little bit at a time while mixing with chopsticks. Note: Depending on where you live, you may need less or more water. I live in a dry climate, so I may use more water than you.
3. The flours start to stick together and eventually it becomes clumps. Using your hands, combine into one ball.
4. Knead until the dough becomes smooth. The texture is like squeezing an "earlobe" (that's how we describe the tenderness for this type of mochi in Japanese).
5. Make the dough into a ball. Divide the dough into 8 equal pieces.
6. Then divide each piece into 2 balls. You will have 16 equal-sized balls. I always like to measure mine. Each ball should be 20 grams. You may have some extra dough, but that's okay.
7. Shape into a nice smooth round ball. If the dough is cracking or has some wrinkles, tap your finger in water and apply a small amount of water on the cracked area to smooth out. I have 16 equal-sized balls.
8. Once the water in the pot is boiling, gently drop each dumpling into the pot <u>with a continuous motion</u>. We want to cook them all at once, but also keeping them in good shapes. Stir the balls occasionally so they don't stick on the bottom of the pot.
9. Dumplings will stay on the bottom first but once they are cooked,

4 Tbsp **sugar**

2 Tbsp **mirin**

2 Tbsp **soy sauce**

150 ml **water** (⅔ cup)

2 Tbsp **potato starch/ cornstarch**

they will float. Then cook an additional 1-2 minute.
10. Transfer the dumplings into iced water.
11. Once the dumplings are cooled, drain well and transfer to a tray (if you wet the tray, the dumplings won't stick).
12. Skewer three pieces into a bamboo skewer. Continue the rest of the balls and set aside.

TO MAKE SWEET SOY GLAZE
1. Combine all the ingredients in a saucepan without turning on the heat.
2. Potato starch/cornstarch will become lumps once you add the heat to it, so mix all together first. Then turn on the heat and continue to whisk.
3. At one point when the sauce gets to hot temperature stage, the sauce will <u>suddenly</u> become thick and heavy. You need to keep whisking.
4. I usually stop at this consistency. If you use it now, then this is a good time to stop cooking. If you are making this sauce ahead, then stop a bit earlier because the sauce will thicken a bit more while it cools down. Transfer to the container or bowl.

TO SERVE
1. [Optional] If you have a kitchen torch, you can give them a little bit of char for taste. You can also grill over the direct heat (If you are going to place on a wire rack, dumplings tend to stick, so grease it). You can use a broiler to give a char or use a non-stick frying pan to pan fry the surface of dango.
2. Pour the sweet soy glaze on top and serve immediately.

TO STORE
1. **Option 1:** After you form the dough into round dumplings, put un- cooked dumplings in a single layer in an airtight container andfreeze up to a month. When you use them, boil the frozen dango without defrosting.
2. **Option 2:** After boiling and cooling down, pat dry and pack into an airtight container without sticking to each other and freeze up to a month. When you use them, microwave or boil till they are warm.

Daifuku

A popular Japanese sweet, Daifuku is a small round mochi stuffed with sweet red bean paste. This recipe shows how you can make this delicious snack at home with quick steam over the stovetop or in the microwave.

 PREP TIME: 30 Minutes   **COOK TIME:** 3 Minutes   Servings: 12 Pieces

Ingredients

¾ cup **shiratamako (glutinous rice flour/ sweet rice flour)** (100 g)

¾ cup **water** (180 ml)

¼ cup **sugar** (50 g)

½ cup **potato starch/cornstarch** (100 g)

1½ cup **red bean paste (anko)** (I use "tsubuan")(480 g)

SUBSTITUTE FOR SHIRATAMAKO:
¾ cup **mochiko (glutinous rice flour/ sweet rice flour)** (115 g)

Instructions

1. Combine shiratamako and sugar in a medium bowl and whisk all together.
2. Add water and mix well until combined.
3. **Microwave Method:** If you're using a microwave to cook mochi, cover the bowl with some plastic wrap (not too tight). Put the bowl in the microwave and heat it on high heat (1100w microwave) for 1 minute. Take it out and stir with a wet rubber spatula. Cover again and cook for 1 minute. Stir again, cover, and cook for 30 seconds to finish cooking. The color of mochi should change from white to almost translucent.
4. **Steaming Method:** Cover the steamer lid with a towel so the condensation won't drop into the mochi mixture. Put the bowl into a steamer basket and cover to cook for 15 minutes. Half way through cooking, stir with a wet rubber spatula and cover to finish cooking. The color of mochi should change from white to almost translucent.
5. Cover the work surface with parchment paper and dust it generously with potato starch. Then transfer the cooked mochi on top.
6. To prevent from sticking, sprinkle more potato starch on top of the mochi. Once it's cool down slightly, you can spread the mochi into a thin layer with your hands or with a rolling pin. Make sure to apply potato starch on your hands and the rolling pin. I recommend using a rolling pin because it's easier to spread out evenly.
7. Transfer the mochi with parchment paper onto a large baking sheet. Refrigerate for 15 minutes until the mochi is set.
8. Take out the mochi from the refrigerator and cut out 7-8 circles with the cookie cutter.
9. Dust off the excess potato starch with a pastry brush. If you find some sticky part, cover the area with potato starch first then dust off. Place a plastic wrap on a plate and then mochi wrapper on top, then lay another layer of plastic wrapper down. Repeat for all wrappers. With leftover

mochi dough, roll into a ball and then flatten into a thin layer again and cut out into more circle wrappers (about 12 mochi wrappers).

10. Now we're ready to make daifuku mochi. On the work surface, place one sheet of plastic wrap with a mochi layer on top. Using the cookie scoop, scoop out anko on top of the mochi wrapper.

11. Pinch the four corners of the mochi layer together to wrap the anko. Then pinch the remaining corners together.

12. Put some potato starch on the sealed area and set aside. Continue making the rest of daifuku mochi. Store in a cool dry place (refrigerator in summer months) and enjoy within two days.

Zenzai (Oshiruko) – Red Bean Soup with Mochi

Nothing sounds better than a warm bowl of homemade Zenzai or Oshiruko (red bean soup) with toasted mochi! I'll show you 3 ways to make this popular winter dessert in Japan.

 PREP TIME: 5 Minutes    **COOK TIME:** 15 Minutes

 Servings: 4 big bowls (or 6 small bowls)

 PRESSURIZING + NATURAL RELEASE TIME: 40 Minutes

Ingredients

USING AZUKI BEANS (MAKES 4-6)

1 cup **azuki beans** (7 oz or 200 g)

4 cups **water** (960 ml)

pinch **kosher/ sea salt** (I use Diamond Crystal; Use half for table salt)

6 oz **sugar** (170 g or ¾ cup; It's sweet enough for me. Typically 150-200 g sugar is used for 200 g azuki beans)

USING STORE-BOUGHT OR HOMEMADE RED

Instructions

MAKING ZENZAI WITH AZUKI BEANS (MAKES 4-6)

OPTION 1: PRESSURE COOKER

1. Rinse the azuki beans carefully until water is clear. Discard any damaged beans that are floating. Drain water and transfer the beans to the pressure cooker (I use an Instant Pot).
2. Add in 4 cups of water. Cover and lock the lid of your pressure cooker. Make sure the steam release handle points at "sealing" and not venting.
3. Turn on your pressure cooker and select High Pressure for **15 minutes** (10 minutes if you prefer to keep the beans slightly firm). If you're using an Instant Pot, press "Manual" or "Pressure Cooker", select "high pressure" and adjust the cooking time.
4. **If you are using a stovetop pressure cooker**, cook on high heat until high pressure is reached. Then reduce the heat to low to maintain the pressure for 15 minutes.
5. When it's done cooking, the Instant Pot will switch automatically to the "Keep Warm" mode. Let the pressure slowly release by itself for 30 minutes (**natural release**). Before opening the lid, turn the steam release handle to "Venting" and release any leftover pressure. **If you're using the stovetop pressure cooker**, remove the pot from the heat and let the pressure release naturally.
6. Add salt and sugar into the pot.
7. Press the "Sauté" button and select "Low" heat. Let the sugar dissolved completely, stirring occasionally, about 5 minutes.
8. After cooking for 5 minutes, the soup will turn slightly darker in color. Keep warm and start preparing the mochi.

BEAN PASTE (ANKO) (MAKES 1)

3.5 oz **red bean paste (anko)** (100 g or roughly ½ cup)

½ cup **water** (120 ml or more if you desire)

a pinch of **kosher/ sea salt** (I use Diamond Crystal; Use half for table salt)

TO SERVE

4 pieces **kirimochi or homemade mochi** (Here's my Homemade Mochi recipe. You can also use my Shiratama Dango recipe for this red bean soup.)

OPTION 2: STOVETOP METHOD

1. Rinse the azuki beans carefully until water is clear. Discard any damaged beans that are floating and drain.
2. Put the azuki beans and water in a pot.
3. Bring the water to a boil over medium-high heat. Once boiling, put an otoshibuta (drop lid) over the azuki beans. Turn down the heat to medium-low and keep it simmering for the next 1 to 1.5 hours. *Tip: Otoshibuta will prevent the beans from dancing around too much. You can make it with aluminum foil.*
4. **Water will evaporate so you need to keep adding water** so the beans are submerged. After 1 hour, pick one bean and mash it with your fingers. If it is mashed easily, it's done. Otherwise, cook another 15 minutes and check. Add sugar and salt and let the sugar dissolved completely, stirring occasionally. Keep warm and start preparing the mochi.

MAKING ZENZAI WITH RED BEAN PASTE (MAKES 1)

1. In a small saucepan, combine the store-bought red bean paste or homemade red bean paste and water and bring it to a boil. Add a pinch of salt and mix well. Adjust the consistency by adding or evaporating water. Keep warm and start preparing the mochi.

TO PREPARE MOCHI AND SERVE

1. Cut the kirimochi into halves or quarters and place them in the toaster oven (or the oven). If you're using the fresh homemade mochi, add it in the soup to warm up. If it's frozen, then boil it in a pot till soft.
2. Toast the mochi until puffed up and nicely brown, about 10-12 minutes.
3. Serve the red bean soup and mochi in a bowl and enjoy!

Japanese Strawberry Shortcake

Moist, airy, and light Japanese strawberry shortcake recipe with homemade whipped cream. This simple and elegant cake is perfect for celebrating all occasions.

 PREP TIME: 2 Hours   **COOK TIME:** 25 Minutes   1 Serving: 8 inch (20 cm) cake

Ingredients

FOR THE
SPONGE CAKE
40 g **unsalted
butter** (3 Tbsp)

30 ml **whole milk**
(2 Tbsp)

4 **large eggs** (50
g each w/o shell)

120 g **sugar** (½
cup + 2 Tbsp)

120 g **cake flour**
(roughly 1 cup)

14 g **butter** (1
Tbsp)

FOR THE SYRUP
30 ml **water** (2
Tbsp)

38 g **sugar** (3
Tbsp)

Instructions

BEFORE WE START

1. Make sure the eggs and butter are at room temperature. Sift the cake flour at least twice.
2. Place the cake pan on top of parchment paper, trace around the pan and cut out the circle. Grease one side of the parchment paper and also both bottom and sides of the cake pan with shortening/cooking spray/butter. Then fit the parchment paper in the cake pan. (I avoid parchment paper on the side because sometimes it pulls the batter and affect the final result of the cake).
3. Preheat oven to 350°F (180°C). If you use a convection oven, preheat to 325°F (160°C). It's always better to preheat longer, preferably 15-20 mins longer.
4. Prepare a double boiler. Turn on the stove's heat to high and bring the water in the saucepan (Pot A) to a rapid boil. When boiling, reduce heat to maintain a steady simmer. Put the 40g (3 Tbsp) of butter in the small bowl (Bowl #1) and set over the saucepan. Let the butter melt gently.
5. Once the butter is melted, remove the bowl from the saucepan. Then add 30 ml (2 Tbsp.) whole milk and whisk to combine. Set aside to keep it around 104°F (40°C).

FOR THE SPONGE CAKE

1. In the stand mixer bowl (Bowl #2), add 4 eggs and break the egg yolks and whites.
2. Add 120 g (½ cup + 2 Tbsp) sugar and whisk to combine.
3. In the large pot (Pot B), bring about 2 inches of water to 140°F or 60°C and maintain the temperature. Then set the stand mixer bowl (Bowl #2) directly in the pot and whisk constantly so the eggs don't become scrambled. This method is called bain marie (or water bath), where the bowl of food is set directly in a larger container of hot or simmering water. You can also use

1 Tbsp **your liquor of choice** (Optional)

FOR THE CREAM
480 ml **heavy (whipping) cream** (2 cups/1 Pint package) (36%, at least 30-35% fat)

38 g **sugar** (3 Tbsp) (use 8% of heavy cream: 473 ml x 8 % = 38g)

FOR DECORATION
450 g **strawberries** (1 lb) (for filling and decoration – buy extra)

10 **blueberries**

mint leaves

the double boiler method, where you set the egg mixture bowl (Bowl #2) over the Pot B. The bowl doesn't touch the simmering water of the pot. In both cases, the water tempers the heat to permit gentle, even cooking.

4. Whisk until the temperature of the egg mixture reaches 104 °F (40 °C). Remove Bowl #2 from Pot B and set it up on the stand mixer with the whisk attachment.

5. Whisk on high speed (level 10) until the mixture is fluffy, for about 2 minutes. The batter should be loose yet thick and glossy.

6. When the batter is pale and fluffy and tripled in volume, slow down to low speed (level 4) for several seconds. Stop and lift up some of the mixture and fold it in, and if the batter stays on top of the mixture, that's "ribbon stage". Remove from the stand mixer.

7. Add half of the flour. Using the whisk, fold gently but thoroughly. Do this by rotating your bowl slowly, and simultaneously moving your whisk in a downward-then-over motion.

8. Add the rest of the flour and fold gently to make sure all the flour is incorporated quickly so your mixture doesn't deflate.

9. Take out 1 (spatula) scoop of the batter from the bowl and add to the butter & milk mixture.

10. Mix very well. We incorporate butter into batter first because fat in butter will deflate the batter if we add the butter directly.

11. Add the mixture back to the batter by pouring over the silicon spatula. This prevents the mixture from deflating the batter and helps disperse the mixture. Gently fold in. When you lift the spatula, the batter should fold down like ribbon.

12. Pour the batter into the center of the cake pan, from right above the cake pan. You want to avoid introducing extra air into the batter at this point. Collect the leftover batter in the bowl and pour around the edges of the cake pan, not the center.

13. Drop the cake pan on the counter to release air bubbles in the batter.

14. In the preheated oven, bake at 350°F (180°C) (or for a convection oven 325°F /160°C) for 20-25 minutes. Check if the sponge cake is done by inserting a skewer in the middle and comes out clean. Meanwhile, move on to the cake assemble prepping stage.

15. As soon as you take out the cake pan from the oven, drop it on the counter to give shock to the cake (so it stops shrinking). Separate the cake from the pan by running a sharp knife or offset spatula around the pan.

16. Take the cake out of the pan by placing the wire rack on top and flipping it over. Immediately remove the parchment paper.

17. Place another wire rack on top and flip it back. The top of the cake is now facing up.

18. Cover the cake with a damp towel until cooled (to keep moisture in the cake). Make sure the towel is thin (not heavy) and squeeze the water out VERY tightly so that it's damp, not wet. I use a thin dish towel. If you keep

the sponge cake for later use, wrap with plastic wrap and keep it in the fridge.

PREPARATION FOR CAKE ASSEMBLY (WHILE THE CAKE IS BAKING)

1. Divide the strawberries into 2 groups, for decoration and for filling. Keep the beautiful, same-sized strawberries for the decoration. Remove the husk and clean the strawberries with damp paper towel (do not wash, as we don't want strawberries to have moisture and become moldy). Slice off the core for all the strawberries.
2. For the strawberries that we use for topping, cut in half. For the strawberries that we use for filling, slice them into ¼ inch (5 mm) slices.
3. To make syrup, in a small bowl (Bowl #3), combine 30 ml (2 Tbsp) water, 38 g (3 Tbsp) sugar, 1 Tbsp liquor, and microwave for 1 minute to dissolve the sugar.

FOR WHIPPING CREAM (WHILE CAKE IS COOLING)

1. Prepare ice bath by placing ice cubes and water in a large bowl (Bowl #4). Place a clean and dry mixing bowl (Bowl #2) over and add 473 ml (1 Pint) heavy cream and 38 g (3 Tbsp) sugar to keep cool.
2. Once cooled, transfer the mixing bowl to the stand mixer and whisk on high speed. The cream will become thicker and smooth. When you lift the whisk out of the cream while it's still liquid, but holds it shape as it drops, then it's ready. Remove the bowl from the stand mixer and put it back in the ice bath.

THE CAKE ASSEMBLY

1. With a serrated knife, slice the middle of the cake horizontally into half. Now you have 2 layers (top and bottom).
2. Place the bottom of the cake on the cake circle. Brush the syrup on top and the sides of the bottom layer. This will keep the sponge cake stay moist.
3. Start to whisk the cream at one location by the edge of the bowl instead of whisking the entire cream. We will be making the whipped cream as we need. With this approach, we can also control the texture of the cream.
4. When the cream reaches "soft peaks", take out the cream and transfer to the bottom of the cake. Soft peaks means when you lift the whisk, the cream will hold its line but the top peaks will be soft and after a second or two will fall back on itself.
5. Spread the whipped cream evenly. If the whipped cream is not enough, whip more and add onto the cake.
6. Place the strawberries on top of the whipped cream. Keep the center area open by not covering with strawberries. This will be easier to cut the cake into slices.
7. Whip the cream again at the edge of the bowl.
8. Transfer the whipped cream to the top of the strawberry layer. Spread just

enough cream to cover the strawberries, do not put too much.

9. Place the top layer of the sponge cake. Brush the syrup on the top and sides of the sponge cake.

10. Whip more cream and place on the top. Place the tip of the offset spatula in the center at 30 degree angle, turn cake turntable toward you to create a smooth top. Lightly cover the sides of the cake with thin layer of the cream.

11. Now add more cream to the side little by little. Place the offset spatula at 90 degree angle and push the turning table away from you.

12. Remove the excess cream from the cake and put back into the bowl.

FOR CAKE DECORATION

1. For a basic decoration, I use Wilton 2A decoration tip. Put the tip in the piping bag and cut off the tip so the metal will show from the bag. Fold the top half of the bag outward.

2. Whip the cream to "stiff peaks". When you lift the whisk, the peaks will hold firm. Put the cream into the piping bag. Once you fill out the bag half way, lift the bag and push the cream down to the tip.

3. Squeeze the pipe to test to make sure the cream comes out smoothly. When you're ready, hold the piping bag at 90 degree angle and squeeze about 1 inch diameter of whipped cream around the edge of the cake. This will be the base for the strawberries.

4. Decorate and place the strawberries sideways on top of the whipped cream. Then squeeze more whipped cream in between strawberries, dropping small whipped cream all around. Place blueberries between the whipped cream dollops. Place the small mint leaves in some area to add colors.

5. Keep the cake in the refrigerator and enjoy it in 2 days.

Castella Cake

Treat yourself with this super moist Japanese sponge cake with a hint of sweetness from honey! Made with only 4 ingredients, Japanese Castella Cake is a very popular confectionary in Japan. Try this delicious cake for your weekend baking project. It makes the perfect holiday or hostess gift too.

 PREP TIME: 25 Minutes   **COOK TIME:** 35 Minutes   Servings: 2 Castella cakes

Ingredients

6 **large eggs** (50 g each w/o shell) (at room temperature - very important!)

200 g **sugar** (1 cup)

200 g **bread flour** (1 ½ cup + 2 ½ Tbsp)

80 ml **honey** (⅓ cup; 5 Tbsp)

2 ½ Tbsp **water** (warm)

HONEY MIXTURE FOR BRUSHING CASTELLA
1 Tbsp **honey**

½ Tbsp **water** (warm)

Instructions

1. I use a KitchenAid stand mixer for this recipe.
2. Cut parchment paper to fit the baking pans.
3. Preheat oven to 320°F (160°C).
4. Sift the bread flour with the sifter or a fine-meshed strainer twice. Holding the handle with one hand and tapping the strainer gently with the other, the flour will gradually sift through the strainer.
5. Add 2 ½ Tbsp warm water to honey and whisk well.
6. Fit the mixer with the whisk attachment. Crack eggs into the bowl and vigorously whisk until combined.
7. Add the sugar.
8. Beat the eggs and sugar on high speed (Speed 10) for 5 minutes. The volume of the beaten eggs will increase about 4 times. The texture will be thick and the color will be pale yellow. When you stop the mixer and lift the whisk attachment, the mixture should fall in ribbons.
9. Add the honey mixture into the egg mixture and whisk on low speed (Speed 2) until combined, about 30 seconds.
10. Add the bread flour at three separate times: add ⅓ of the bread flour and whisk on low speed (Speed 2) for 15 seconds, then add more flour and whisk for 15 seconds. Add the last remaining portion and whisk until just combined for about 1 minute. Do not overmix.
11. Spray the loaf pans with oil and spread out evenly with pastry brush.
12. Put the parchment paper in the pans and make sure the paper sticks to the pans. If not, add oil and spread out evenly with a brush.
13. Pour the batter into the pans (about 80% full).
14. Using a skewer, draw a zigzag line to remove the air bubbles in the batter.
15. Level batter in each pan by holding pan 2-inches above counter dropping it flat onto the counter. Do this several times to release air bubbles.
16. Bake at 320°F (160°C) in the middle rack of the oven for 35 to 40 minutes, or until golden brown and a skewer inserted in the center comes out clean.

I bake for 35 minutes and keep my oven door ajar for a few minutes then I take out the cake. When done, cake sides will pull away from the pan slightly; the top will be flat and feel spongy when pressed with a finger.

17. Mix 1 Tbsp honey and ½ Tbsp warm water in a bowl and apply the honey mixture on top of the cake with a pastry brush.

18. Place a sheet of plastic wrap on the counter top. Take out the cake from the pan to the plastic wrap, top facing down. Gently peel off parchment paper.

19. Immediately wrap the cake with plastic wrap to keep the moisture and while it's hot store in the refrigerator overnight (at least 12 hours), keeping the top side facing down. This gives the cake a more fine and moist texture.

20. To serve, slice off the sides of the cake with a sharp bread knife and cut into ¾ to 1 inch thick slices (you get 7-8 slices total). It's better if you bring the cake to room temperature before serving.

TO STORE

To save for later, wrap individual pieces with plastic wrap. You can store at room temperature for up to 3-4 days, 5-7 days in the refrigerator, and 1 month in the freezer.

Steamed Cake (Mushi-pan)

Making these soft, light, spongy Japanese steamed cake (Mushi-pan) is surprisingly easy. You can enjoy them as a healthy breakfast or after-school snack. Choose savory or sweet based on the ingredients you use.

 PREP TIME: 10 Minutes   **COOK TIME:** 10 Minutes   Servings: 4 Steamed cakes

Ingredients

FOR BASIC STEAMED CAKE

½ cup **all-purpose flour** (plain flour) (60 g)

1 tsp **baking powder**

1 **large egg** (50 g w/o shell)

2 Tbsp **milk**

2 Tbsp **sugar**

1 Tbsp **neutral-flavored oil** (vegetable, canola, etc)

FOR CORN & CHEESE STEAMED CAKE:

½ cup **all-purpose flour** (plain flour) (60 g)

1 tsp **baking powder**

1 **large egg** (50 g w/o shell)

Instructions

Cover the lid with a kitchen towel to prevent condensation (**please don't skip!**). Fill a large frying pan with water about ½ inch (1.3 cm) deep. Cover the pan with the lid and slowly bring water to a boil. **STEAMER:** You can also use a regular steamer, but the cooking time will be slightly longer than my method here. **Please read the storage and reheating information at the end of the recipe.**

FOR BASIC STEAMED CAKE

1. Gather all the ingredients. You will also need 4 6-oz ramekins and cupcake liners.
2. In a medium bowl, combine all-purpose flour and baking powder and whisk well to combine (shortcut for sifting).
3. In a small bowl, whisk the egg, milk, sugar, and vegetable oil together until combined and sugar is dissolved.
4. Pour the egg mixture into the flour mixture and mix until just combined and smooth. Don't over mix.
5. Put a cupcake liner in glass ramekins and divide the batter into the cupcake liners.
6. Place the glass ramekins in the boiling water and cook covered on the lowest heat for 8 minutes.
7. They're done when a skewer inserted comes out clean without wet batter. Turn off the heat and remove the ramekins from the pan and let them cool on a wire rack. Serve warm or at room temperature.

FOR CORN & CHEESE STEAMED CAKE

1. In a medium bowl, combine all-purpose flour and baking powder and whisk well to combine (shortcut for sifting).
2. In a small bowl, whisk the egg, milk, sugar, and vegetable oil together until combined and sugar is dissolved.

2 Tbsp **milk**

2 Tbsp **sugar**

1 Tbsp **neutral-flavored oil** (vegetable, canola, etc)

¼ cup **corn kernels** (40 g)

¼ cup **shredded cheese** (25 g) (I used sharp cheddar)

FOR DOUBLE CHOCOLATE STEAMED CAKE:
½ cup **all-purpose flour** (plain flour) (60 g)

1 tsp **baking powder**

1½ Tbsp **unsweetened cocoa powder** (7 g)

1 large egg (50 g w/o shell)

3 Tbsp **milk**

2 Tbsp **sugar**

2 Tbsp **neutral-flavored oil** (vegetable, canola, etc)

2 Tbsp **chocolate chips** (25 g)

3. Pour the egg mixture into the flour mixture and mix until just combined and smooth. Don't over mix.
4. Add corn and cheese and mix until combined. Put a cupcake liner in glass ramekins and divide the batter into the cupcake liners.
5. Place the glass ramekins in the boiling water and cook covered on the lowest heat for 12-13 minutes. They're done when a skewer inserted comes out clean without wet batter.
6. Turn off the heat and remove the ramekins from the pan and let them cool on a wire rack. Serve warm or at room temperature.

FOR DOUBLE CHOCOLATE STEAMED CAKE
1. In a medium bowl, combine all-purpose flour, baking powder and cocoa powder, and whisk well to combine (shortcut for sifting).
2. In a small bowl, whisk the egg, milk, sugar, and vegetable oil together until combined and sugar is dissolved.
3. Pour the egg mixture into the flour mixture and mix until just combined and smooth. Don't over mix.
4. Add chocolate chips and mix until combined. Put a cupcake liner in glass ramekins and divide the batter into the cupcake liners.
5. Place the glass ramekins in the boiling water and cook covered on the lowest heat for 8 minutes. They're done when a skewer inserted comes out clean without wet batter. Turn off the heat and remove the ramekins from the pan and let them cool on a wire rack. Serve warm or at room temperature.

TO STORE & REHEAT
You can store the steamed cakes in the airtight container for up to 2-3 days or freeze them for up to 1 month. You can reheat the steamed cake with one of 2 methods. 1) Cover the steamed cake with a damp paper towel and reheat in the microwave (but be careful not to overheat; it'll become very hard). If you reheat the frozen steamed cake, defrost first before microwaving. 2) Use the same steaming method above or a steamer or to reheat refrigerated/frozen steamed cake till warm.

Green Tea Chiffon Cake

Made with eggs, sugar, vegetable oil, cake flour, and green tea powder, this matcha green tea chiffon cake is moist and spongy. Perfect for a light afternoon snack!

 PREP TIME: 20 Minutes   **COOK TIME:** 30 Minutes

 1 Serving: 17-cm (about 7 inch) cake

Ingredients

3 **large egg yolks**

85 g **sugar** (3 oz or ½ cup and take away 1 Tbsp)

3 Tbsp **neutral-flavored oil** (vegetable, canola, etc)

4 Tbsp **water** (60 ml)

75 g **cake flour** (⅔ cup and remove 2 tsp; If you're using a cup measurement, please follow this method to measure. Otherwise, the amount of flour tends to be more than you need. You can make your Homemade Cake Flour.)

1 heaping Tbsp

Instructions

1. Preheat oven to 340°F (170°C). You will also need a 17cm (7") chiffon cake pan. Make sure you use the correct chiffon cake pan. The best types are the aluminum ones with a removable base (Do not use non-stick bakeware for chiffon cake – it will not work). Do not grease the mold because the cake needs to cling on the sides and center of the pan for support as it rises or it will collapse.

2. In a large bowl, whisk egg yolks and add ⅓ of the sugar. Then add oil and water and whisk all together till combined.

3. Sift cake flour, matcha, and baking powder together and add to the egg yolk mixture in 3 separate times. Whisk until totally incorporated and make sure there are no lumps.

4. Using a stand mixer, whip the egg whites on medium-low speed (speed 4) till opaque and foamy and bubbly.

5. Add ⅓ of the remaining sugar and continue whipping. After 30 seconds or so, increase the stand mixer speed to high (speed 10) and add the remaining sugar slowly in small increments. It takes about 2 minutes (since you changed the speed to speed 10) until stiff peaks form.

6. To check on stiff peaks, pull up your whisk and see if the egg whites go straight up (stiff peak) and just the tip is soft enough that it folds over, like taking a bow.

7. Add ⅓ of the beaten egg whites into the flour mixture using spatula until the mixture is homogeneous.

8. Fold in the rest of the egg whites in 2-3 increments and mix gently but quickly until the mixture is homogeneous.

9. Pour the mixture into the ungreased 17cm (7") chiffon cake pan. Tap the pan a few times on the kitchen countertop to release the air bubbles.

10. Bake for 30 minutes or until a toothpick inserted comes out clean.

matcha (green tea powder) (about 10 g or 0.4 oz)

1 tsp **baking powder**

3 large **egg whites**

11. The cake must be cooled upside down; stick the pan on a tall heavy bottle, leave until the cake is completely cool before removing it from the pan.
12. Use a thin sharp knife or thin offset spatula and run it around the cake.
13. Place the serving plate on top and flip over. The cake will pop out easily. Enjoy!

Green Tea Cookies

Enjoy your afternoon tea with these buttery, crispy Green Tea Cookies with Matcha powder. The unique flavor of matcha in the cookies is surprisingly delightful!

 PREP TIME: 20 Minutes   **COOK TIME:** 15 Minutes   Servings: 24 cookies

Ingredients

240 g **all-purpose flour** (plain flour) (2 cups; If you're using a cup measurement, please follow this method to measure. Otherwise, the amount of flour tends to be more than you need.)

15 g **matcha green tea powder** (2 ½ Tbsp; 1 Tbsp matcha is 6 g)

170 g **unsalted butter** (¾ cup; softened)

130 g **confectioners' sugar/powdered sugar** (roughly 1 cup)

a pinch of **kosher/ sea salt** (I use Diamond Crystal; Use half for table salt)

Instructions

1. Combine 240 g (2 cups) all-purpose flour and 15 g (2 ½ Tbsp) matcha green tea powder in a large bowl.
2. Sift the flour and the matcha powder.
3. In a stand mixer with the paddle attachment or in a large bowl with a hand mixer, beat 170 g (¾ cup) unsalted butter until smooth and creamy. It's important to soften the butter ahead of time.
4. Add a pinch of salt and blend.
5. Add 130 g (roughly 1 cup) powdered sugar and blend until soft and light. Scrape down the bowl as needed.
6. Add 2 large egg yolks and mix well until combined.
7. Gradually add the flour and matcha green tea powder mix and blend until the dough is smooth.
8. Add 50 g (¼ cup) white chocolate chips and blend well.
9. Cut the dough in half and shape into 2 cylinders, about 1.5 inches (4 cm) diameter, 7" (18 cm) long.
10. Wrap the logs in plastic wrap and chill in the refrigerator until firm, at least 2 hours (or overnight). Optional: you can place the logs on a bed of rice while chilling. It'll keep the dough in a nice cylindrical shape, so your cookie slices won't be flat on one side.
11. Preheat the oven to 350°F (175°C). Line the baking sheet with parchment paper or silicone baking liner. Remove the dough from the plastic wrap, and with a sharp knife, slice the dough into ⅓ inches (7 mm) thick rounds. Place them on the baking sheet, leaving about 1" (2.5 cm) between rounds.
12. Bake the cookies at 350°F (175°C) for about 15 minutes, or until the edge of the cookies starts to get slightly golden brown.
13. Remove from the oven and let cool on the baking sheet for 5 minutes; then carefully transfer to a cooling rack and let cool completely. If you pack the cookies in an airtight container, they will keep for at least 4 days.

2 **large egg yolks**

50 g **white chocolate chips** (¼ cup)

14. You can also freeze the unbaked logs of dough, wrapped in plastic wrap, for up to 2 months. Let sit at room temperature for about 10 minutes before cutting and baking. Do not let the dough fully defrost.

Miso Butter Cookies

Crisp, buttery, and melt-in-your-mouth, these Miso Butter Cookies make the most insanely delicious afternoon treat! They hit the right notes with a serious depth of flavor. Only 7 pantry ingredients needed!

 PREP TIME: 20 Minutes   **COOK TIME:** 20 Minutes   Servings: 32 cookies

Ingredients

½ cup **unsalted butter** (1 stick, 113 g; softened to room temperature; you can microwave the cold stick of butter for 5 seconds each side, total of 20 seconds)

½ cup **sugar** (100 g)

2 Tbsp **miso** (40 g; I use mild and mellow white miso; If you use a different type of miso, your cookies will have a slightly different taste and color. Reduce the amount if you're using Dashi-Included Miso or Red Miso as they are saltier.)

1 **large egg** (50 g w/o shell) (at room temperature; you can soak the eggs in

Instructions

1. In a large bowl, using a handheld mixer or a stand mixer fitted with a paddle attachment, beat the butter for 30 seconds.
2. Add ½ cup sugar and 2 Tbsp miso.
3. Beat everything together on medium-high speed until smooth, light, and fluffy, about 2 minutes.
4. Crack the egg and whisk in a small bowl. Gradually add the egg to the butter mixture while mixing.
5. Beat on high speed until combined, about 1 minute. Scrape down the sides and up the bottom of the bowl and beat again as needed to combine in between.
6. In a small bowl, combine 1 ⅔ cup all-purpose flour and 1 tsp baking powder and mix with a fork (I do this extra step so that baking powder is evenly distributed when sifting).
7. With a fine-mesh sieve, sift the flour mixture over a medium bowl.
8. Gradually add the flour mixture into the mixing bowl at low speed.
9. Once you finish adding all the flour mixture, turn up to high speed and beat until incorporated.
10. Sprinkle a small amount of flour on the working surface and transfer the dough. If the dough is too soft, chill in the refrigerator for 15 minutes. By chilling, the butter/fat will solidify and it'll be easier to work with.
11. Roll the dough into a ball and cut in half. Note: This recipe can be used for cut out cookies. Form the dough into a disk, wrap and chill then roll out to ¼-½ inch, cut and bake.
12. Roll the dough into 2 long logs.
13. Each log should be 10 inches (25 cm) long with 1 inch (2.5 cm) diameter.
14. Cut the long logs in half; now you have four 5-inch (12.5 cm) logs.
15. Prepare a small flat container (or baking sheet) and add white sesame

warm water to bring to room temp)

1 ⅔ cup **all-purpose flour** (200 g; if you use a measuring cup, fluff your flour with a spoon, sprinkle it into your measuring cup, and use a knife to level it off. Otherwise, your flour ends up with more than 200 g.)

1 tsp **baking powder**

3 Tbsp **toasted white sesame seeds**

3 Tbsp **toasted black sesame seeds**

seeds (save the black one for later). Moist a sheet of paper towel with water and wrap around the log so the dough is moistened.

16. Roll the moistened log in the sesame seeds and wrap in parchment paper or plastic.

17. I've learned the best way to keep the dough from flattening out on the bottom is to place the dough on rice.

18. Roll the other 2 logs in the black sesame seeds and wrap in parchment paper or plastic.

19. Chill the cookie dough in the refrigerator for at least 30 minutes. Meanwhile, preheat oven to 350°F (180°C). Prepare a baking sheet lined with parchment paper.

20. Once the dough is chilled, use a sharp knife to cut dough into 8 slices of even thickness.

21. Cut the rest of the cookie dough and transfer to the baking sheet lined with parchment paper. If the dough is no longer chilled, you can put the baking sheet in the refrigerator for 15 minutes until the cookies are chilled and firm. Tip: If the cookie dough is chilled, they will not completely lose their shape.

22. Bake the chilled cookies for 20-22 minutes or until lightly browned on the edges.

23. Remove from the oven and allow to cool on the baking sheet for 5 minutes before transferring to a wire rack to cool completely.

TO STORE

These cookies stay fresh in an airtight container at room temperature for up to 1 week. I usually reheat the cookies at 350 °F (180 °C) in the toaster oven (or oven) until toasty. To freeze the dough: Tightly wrap the logs in plastic wrap and put them into freezer bags. Freeze for up to 3 months. Let them thaw in the refrigerator for 2 hours before slicing.

HOMEMADE
CONDIMENTS & SAUCES

Unagi Sauce

Sweet, savory, and full of flavor, this delicious Homemade Unagi Sauce is the dream sauce for eel and BBQ dishes!

 COOK TIME: 20 Minutes   Servings: 100 ml (a bit less than ½ cup)

Ingredients

¼ cup **mirin**

1 ½ Tbsp **sake**

2 ½ Tbsp **sugar**

¼ cup **soy sauce**

Instructions

1. In a small saucepan, add mirin, sake, sugar. Turn on the heat to medium and whisk all the mixture.
2. Then add soy sauce and bring it to a boil. Once boiling, reduce heat to the low and continue simmering for 10 minutes. Toward the end of cooking, you will see more bubbles.
3. Turn off the heat and let cool. The sauce will thicken more as it cools.

TO STORE

You can store the sauce in an airtight jar and keep in the refrigerator for up to 2-3 months.

How To Make Japanese Curry Roux

Learn how to make Japanese Curry Roux from scratch. Only 5 ingredients! This easy recipe will have you cook up many delicious pots of Japanese curry.

 PREP TIME: 5 Minutes   **COOK TIME:** 25 Minutes

 Servings: 1 yields ⅓ cup roux; enough for your curry recipe that requires 3-4 cups of liquid. If not sure, make a double as everyone prefers different consistency for curry.

Ingredients

3 Tbsp **unsalted butter**

4 Tbsp **all-purpose flour** (plain flour) (use gluten free flour for GF) (30 g)

1 Tbsp **curry powder** (I use Japanese S&B curry powder or curry powder from a local Indian grocery store.)

1 Tbsp **garam masala**

¼ tsp **cayenne pepper** (optional for spicy)

Instructions

1. In a small saucepan, melt the butter over low heat.
2. When the butter is completely melted, add the flour. Stir to combine the butter and flour.
3. Soon the butter and flour fuse and swell. Keep stirring because the roux will easily burn. Cook for 15-20 minutes on low heat.
4. The roux will become light brown color.
5. Add the garam masala, curry powder, and cayenne pepper.
6. Cook and stir for 30 seconds and remove from the heat. Use the curry roux in your curry recipe. Make sure to taste and season with salt after you add the roux to the dish (as the roux is not salted).

TO STORE

If you don't use it immediately, let it cool in an airtight container with lid and store in the refrigerator for a month or freezer for 3-4 months.

Spicy Mayo

Here's a super easy way to make Spicy Mayo. Creamy, tangy with a delicious kick of spice, this wonder sauce is so good on everything!

 PREP TIME: 1 Minute   Servings: 1

Ingredients

1 Tbsp **Japanese mayonnaise**

1 tsp **sriracha sauce**

Instructions

Combine mayo and sriracha sauce in a bowl and mix well. Ta da! It's that simple.

Kombu Tsukudani

Cooked in a sweet and savory sauce, Kombu Tsukudani (Simmered Kombu) is a delicious way to use up the leftover kombu. It makes a great side dish to accompany your ordinary steamed rice!

 PREP TIME: 10 Minutes   **COOK TIME:** 30 Minutes   Servings: 1

Ingredients

2 oz **used kombu (kelp)** (I used Hidaka Kombu from making dashi; Hidaka Kombu is tender and easy to cook while Ma Kombu and Rishiri Kombu are thick and hard to cook. Check out the different types of kombu.)(55 g)

½ tsp **sesame seeds**

SEASONINGS
1 cup **water** (240 ml)

1 Tbsp **sake**

1 Tbsp **mirin**

1 tsp **rice vinegar**

2 Tbsp **soy sauce**

1 tsp **sugar** (add more if you prefer the sweet taste)

½ tsp **katsuobushi (dried bonito flakes)**

1 **dried red chili pepper**

Instructions

1. Cut the kombu into thin strips.
2. Remove the seeds from the dried red chili pepper and cut the pepper into thin rounds.
3. Transfer the kombu into a medium saucepan. Add water, mirin, and sake.
4. Add rice vinegar, soy sauce, sugar, and katsuobushi.
5. Add the red chili pepper and bring the liquid to a boil over medium heat.
6. Once boiling, reduce heat to low and simmer until the liquid is almost evaporated, about 20-25 minutes. If kombu is still not tender, add water and continue to cook.
7. Sprinkle sesame seeds and ready to serve.

TO STORE
Keep the Tsukudani in the refrigerate and consume within 2 weeks.

Homemade Furikake

Homemade furikake rice seasoning made with kombu and katsuobushi. This quintessential Japanese rice seasoning is fabulous on rice of course, but also on onigiri, udon noodles, soup, salad, popcorn and more.

 PREP TIME: 5 Minutes   **COOK TIME:** 10 Minutes   Servings: 1 cup

Ingredients

½ oz **reserved kombu** (from making dashi or mentsuyu)(15 g)

1 oz **reserved katsuobushi** (from making dashi or mentsuyu; slightly moist)(30 g)

1 Tbsp **toasted white sesame seeds**

2 tsp **toasted black sesame seeds**

nori seaweed (I like seasoned nori (Ajitsuke Nori) or Korean seaweed)

SEASONINGS
1 tsp **sugar** (add more to your taste)

2 tsp **soy sauce** (You can skip adding soy sauce if you use kombu and katsuobushi from making mentsuyu (noodle base soup).)

¼ tsp **kosher/sea salt** (I use Diamond Crystal; Use half for table salt) (add more to your taste)

Instructions

1. Make sure the kombu and katsuobushi are well drained.
2. Cut kombu into small pieces. You can cut katsuobushi into smaller pieces if you prefer.
3. Put kombu and katsuobushi in a saucepan and cook on medium-low heat until katsuobushi becomes dry and separated from each other.
4. Add sugar, salt, and soy sauce.
5. Cook on medium-low heat until the liquid is completely evaporated, and katsuobushi is dehydrated and crispy.
6. Transfer the furikake to a tray or plate and let cool. Once it's cooled, you can add toasted/roasted sesame seeds and nori seaweed.
7. Put in a mason jar or airtight container and enjoy sprinkling over steamed rice and popcorn! You can refrigerate for up to 2 weeks and freeze for up to a month.

Negi Miso (Leek and Miso Sauce)

Negi Miso (Leek and Miso Sauce) is an excellent all-purpose sauce to marinate your meat, dip your vegetables in, season ingredients, or enjoy with steamed rice! With a bright aromatic and savory flavor, it could literally work wonder in any recipes, especially Japanese or Asian dishes.

 PREP TIME: 5 Minutes   **COOK TIME:** 10 Minutes   Servings: 1 cup (240ml)

Ingredients

2 **negi (long green onion)** (2 oz, 60 g; Use 1 negi if it's thick. You can substitute negi with 4-5 scallions/green onions, OR substitute negi with leeks for the texture and scallion/green onion for the flavor.)

1 Tbsp **sesame oil (roasted)**

SEASONINGS
5 Tbsp **miso** (100 g)

2 Tbsp **sugar**

2 Tbsp **mirin**

2 Tbsp **sake**

½ tsp **soy sauce**

Instructions

1. Cut the negi into small pieces.
2. In a medium saucepan or frying pan, add sesame oil and then negi.
3. Sauté the negi until wilted.
4. Add all the seasonings in the pan.
5. Mix well and bring it to boil. Once boiling, reduce the heat and continue to simmer until the sauce gets thicken.
6. When you can see the trail at the bottom of the pan when you draw a line with a spatula, it's done. Transfer the sauce to a sterilized jar.

TO STORE
This sauce can be preserved up to 1 week in the fridge and 2 months in the freezer.

ADDITIONAL COOKING TIPS

Hana Renkon

Here's how to make Hana Renkon, flower-shape lotus root:

Tazuna Konnyaku

Tazuna means "reins" in Japanese. You can use Tazuna Konnyaku in dishes like Oden and Chikuzenni.

Chopsticks in Oil

If you don't have a thermometer, put a wooden chopstick in the oil. If you see bubbles start to appear around the chopstick, it's ready for deep frying.

 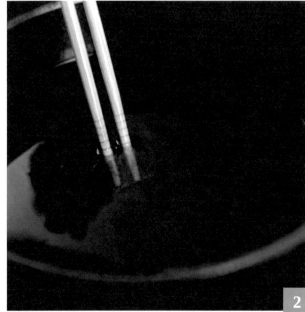

Degrit Clams

Place a wire rack/sieve inside a large tray/bowl and put the clams in a single layer. This way any sand and grit the clams purge would stay on the bottom of the tray/bowl instead of being consumed by the clams again.

Combine 6 cups water and 3 Tbsp salt (I tripled the ingredients) in a large bowl and mix well until salt is completely dissolved.

Pour saltwater into the tray/bowl. The saltwater level should be right around the clam's mouth. If there isn't enough salt water then make more using the same ratio of water and salt. Cover the top with aluminum foil leaving some space at the corner for air. Keep it in a cool dark place (or fridge) for 3 hours. This should give the clams enough time to purge sand and grit.

After 3 hours, take out the sieve and drain the dirty water. Clean clams with a brush under cold water.

Put the clams in clean cold water and set aside for 1 hour to de-salt. Without this process, clams can taste too salty from the saltwater. Drain the clams. The clams are now ready for cooking.

How To Drain Tofu

Wrap the tofu with a paper towel and place it between two baking sheets or plates. Then put a heavy object on top in order to press and drain water from tofu for 15-20 minutes.

How To Julienne Leeks (Shiraga Negi)

Follow these simple instructions on how to slice Negi (Japanese long green onion) into Shiraga Negi (white thin strips) for garnish.

How to Slice Gobo

For certain dishes like tonjiru, here is how I slice gobo.

Scrape the gobo skin with the back of your knife. The flavor of the gobo is right underneath the skin; therefore, you will only need to scrape off the outer skin. Do not use a peeler.

From the end of gobo, make a cross incision about 1 inch deep. This helps "sharpening" the gobo easier. Rotate as you shave the end of the gobo, like how you sharpen a pencil with a knife. Soak the shaved gobo in water to prevent discoloring.

Discard the dirty water and rinse gobo with running water.

Devein Shrimp/Prawns

Pull off the head if it is still attached. Pull off the outer shell.

This will lift up the vein and you can pull off the vein with the skewer or with your hand. If the vein is broken, then insert again a bit lower towards the tail. If you can't find the vein, then don't worry about it.

Devein the back of shrimp with a skewer. The vein runs right along the back. Insert the tip of the skewer sideways about ½ inch down from the head of the shrimp and pull the skewer tip up towards you.

Clean the shrimp with a pinch of salt, 1 Tbsp potato/corn starch, and 2 Tbsp water in a bowl and rub until you see dirty water. Rinse until clean.

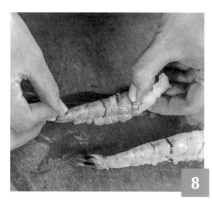

Optional for deep fry recipes: Remove dirty water in the tail by holding the tip of the knife down on the tail and moving it from left to right squeezing the water out from the cut tip. If you skip this process, water retained in the tail might create splatter in the oil. Hold the shrimp with both hands and straighten it as much as possible in order to get the desired shape.

Flower Carrot

Here are the steps to make flower carrot.

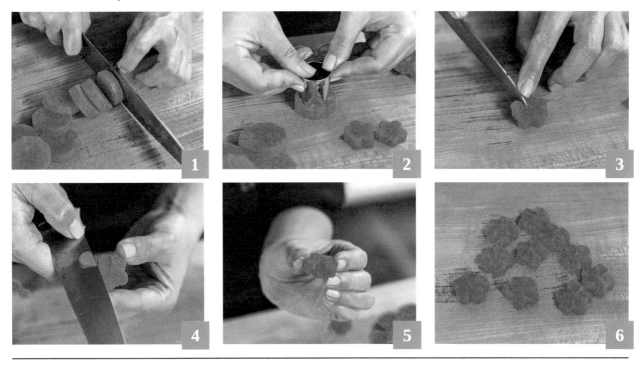

Shiitake Mushroom Decorative Cut

Here are a few ways to decorate shiitake mushrooms.

Japanese Cutting Techniques

Rangiri - Random Shape Cut

Sogigiri - Angle Slicing Cut

Mentori - Remove the corners so that there are no sharp edges

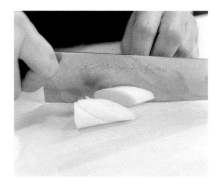

Nanamegiri – Diagonal Cut

Kushigatagiri – Comb Shape Cut

Hangetsugiri – Half Moon Cut

Japanese Kitchen Tools

Ceramic Ginger Grater

Fine Mesh Sieve

Long Chopsticks

Miso Muddler and Strainer

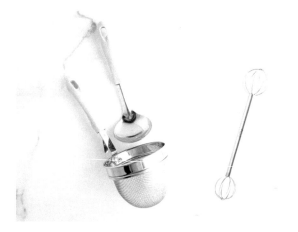

Otoshibuta Drop Lid

Wood Skewers

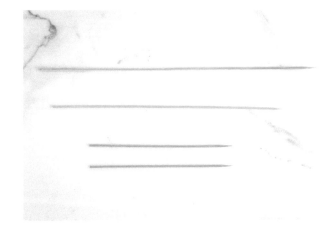

Steamer Basket

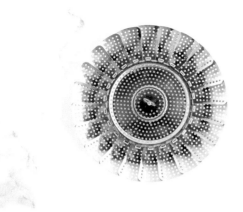

Suribachi Mortar and Pestle

Sushi Mat

Wood Sushi Oke

Where to Buy Japanese & Asian Ingredients Online

It's not always easy to find Japanese ingredients and groceries. Here is a list of online stores that I use and readers have submitted over the years.

UNITED STATES

- Amazon
- 99 Ranch Market
- True fish (formerly ABS Seafood) San Francisco – Sashimi and seafood
- Asian Food Grocer
- Asian Veggies (NYC) – Asian vegetables. Delivery to NYC and part of New Jersey
- Catalina Offshore Products – Sashimi and seafood
- Crowd Cow – Premium Seafood such as salmon, wild Alaskan king crab, and high-quality meat such as wagyu beef and heritage tenderloin
- Dainobu – Japanese online grocery store
- Good Eggs – Japanese fresh produces (Japanese cucumbers, shiso, komatsuna, etc)
- Gold Mine Natural Foods
- HMart
- JustAsianFood.com
- Kitazawa Seed Company – Have a garden at home? This company offers a wide selection of Asian seeds where you can grow mizuna, mitsuba, shiso, shishito peppers, etc.
- Midoriya NYC – Currently deliver to NYC
- MTC Kitchen Home – home delivery in NYC and LA
- Natural Imports
- Pacific Mercantile Company
- Rakuten Japan Spot – Japanese snacks, packaged food, condiments
- SFMart.com – Offers a wide range of Korean, Japanese, and Chinese ingredients and ships all over the US.
- The Japanese Pantry – Curated Japanese ingredients
- Umami Insider – Ships all over US and Canada
- Weee!
- Yamibuy – Offers a wide range of Japanese and Asian ingredients and products

CANADA

- Konbiniya Japan Center – Besides local delivery in Calgary, this Japanese grocery store also offers shipping to Calgary and Alberta.
- Eden Foods – This company offers a variety of Japanese ingredients such as soba, udon, miso, umeboshi, kombu, nori sheet, etc. The website provides information on online retailers that carry their products.
- T&T Supermarket – The shop focuses more on Chinese ingredients, but you can find a variety of Asian products and fresh produce.
- Umami Insider – Ships all over the US and Canada

AUSTRALIA

· **Fuji Mart** – It offers local delivery in Melbourne.

UK

· **Japan Centre**
· **Starry Mart**
· **Wai Yee Hong**
· **Oriental Mart**
· **souschef.co.uk**
· **japan-foods.co.uk**
· **asiangroceryuk.com**

JAPAN

· **Nihon Ichiban**

BELGIUM

· **pimenton.be** – The online shop carries a wide selection of ingredients for world cuisine, but you'll be able to find some essential Japanese products such as soy sauce, togarashi pepper, sake, seaweed, Kewpie mayo, soba noodles and more.

BULGARIA

· **Alex Fish** – They also have a physical store.
· **Tako Foods**

UNITED ARAB EMIRATES

· **Gourmet-ya** (Online delivery in Dubai, Dubai International Airport and Abu Dhabi)
· **El Mart** – Online delivery for frozen Japanese and Asian foods in Dubai

Local Japanese & Asian Grocery Stores in Your City

Looking for local Japanese/Asian grocery stores in your city? Check out the list for **grocery stores around the world** on Just One Cookbook provided by local JOC readers. Some of the shops also provide local delivery, so it's worth looking them up!

RECIPE INDEX

16896405R00176